THE TAFF VALE RAILWAY

Volume 1

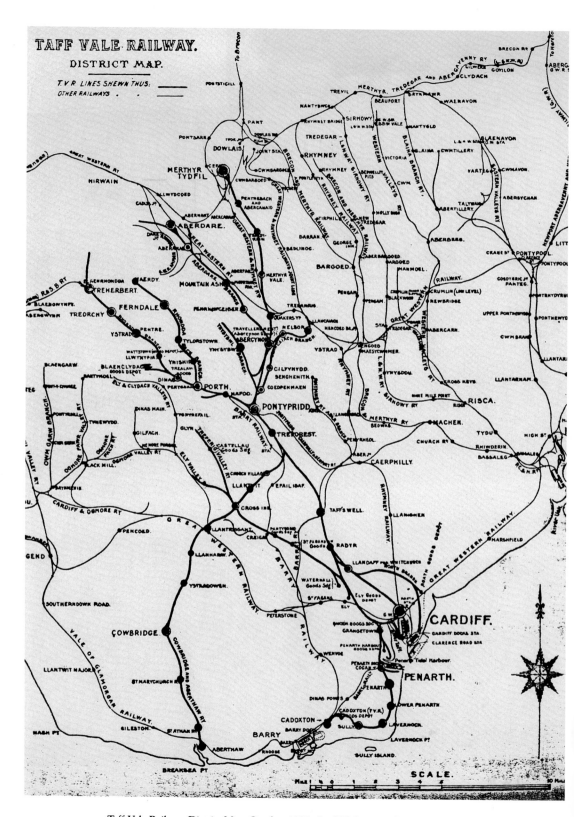

Taff Vale Railway, District Map, October 1903. *Cardiff Libraries and Information Services*

THE
TAFF VALE
RAILWAY

Volume 1
The main line from Cardiff to Merthyr,
and Bute West and East Docks, Cardiff

John Hutton

·RAILWAY HERITAGE·
from
The NOSTALGIA Collection

This work is dedicated to my daughter Nicola, her partner Stephen,
and my granddaughter Chloe

© John Hutton 2006

First published in 2006

British Library Cataloguing in
Publication Data

A catalogue record for this book is
available from the British Library.

ISBN 1 85794 249 3
ISBN 978 1 85794 249 1

Silver Link Publishing Ltd
The Trundle
Ringstead Road
Great Addington
Kettering
Northants NN14 4BW

Tel/Fax: 01536 330588
email: sales@nostalgiacollection.com
Website: www.nostalgiacollection.com

Printed and bound in Great Britain

A Silver Link book
from
The NOSTALGIA *Collection*

The seal of the Taff Vale Railway was photographed at the GWR Museum,
Swindon, where those of other railway companies also taken over by or
amalgamated into the Great Western Railway were also to be seen. *Photograph taken
by permission of the National Railway Museum, York*

CONTENTS

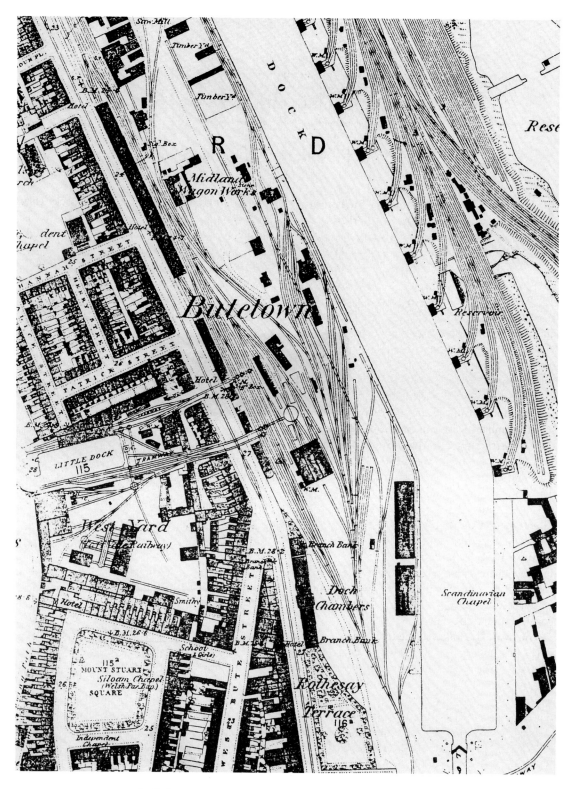

An Ordnance Survey map of 1882 showing part of Bute West Dock,
the TVR's Bute Road station and West Yard. *Crown copyright*

FOREWORD

by Alun Powell, retired railwayman

It gives me great pleasure to write the Foreword for this, the first book in a trilogy that complements John Hutton's *Taff Vale Miscellany*, published in 1988. Since that time Mr Hutton has gained many additional photographs and much additional information regarding the history of the Taff Vale Railway, so much so that not one but three volumes are needed to cover the whole TVR area in a broader aspect than hitherto. This first volume deals entirely with the main line, Cardiff to Merthyr, the West and East Bute Docks, staff, bridges and signal boxes.

In the early part of 1835, Arthur Hill, owner of the Plymouth Iron Works, Merthyr, asked his friend Isambard Kingdom Brunel to estimate the cost constructing a railway from Merthyr to Cardiff, and the figure was £190,649. A meeting was held at the Castle Hotel, Merthyr, where it was decided to promote a company for that purpose, and, despite opposition from the Glamorgan Canal Company, the Taff Vale Railway Company's Act received Royal Assent on 21 June 1836, so incorporating the first public railway of any commercial importance in the principality. The Act protected the Glamorgan Canal from being interfered with by the construction of the railway.

The main line followed the river valley for most of the way, except between Navigation House and Quakers Yard, that section being a very steep incline at 1 in 19 and 1 in 20, which forced Brunel to use stationary winding engines; this arrangement continued until 1864, when an easier route was constructed alongside, with an incline of 1 in 40.

In laying the main line, Brunel decided on 4ft 8½in rather than his usual 7ft 'broad gauge', and the first section of 16 miles from Cardiff to Abercynon (then called Navigation House) opened to traffic in 1840. In 1841 the line was extended to Merthyr,

the original stations being Cardiff Docks (later Bute Road), Llandaff, Pentyrch (later Radyr, further south), Taffs Well (first site), Newbridge (later renamed Pontypridd), Navigation House (later Abercynon), TroedyRhiw, and Merthyr.

The TVR station at Merthyr was situated on the south side of the town, between the River Taff and the Cardiff Road (the suffix Plymouth Street was added when the Vale of Neath Railway opened its Merthyr High Street Station on 2 November 1853). The Cardiff terminus was near the Ship

Act of Parliament for the Taff Vale Railway, dated 21 June 1836. *Cardiff Libraries and Information Services*

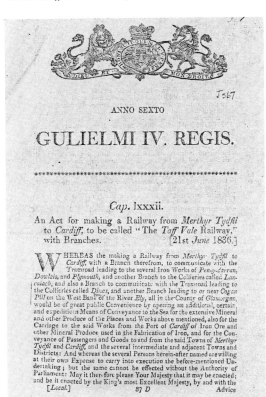

J567

ANNO SEXTO

GULIELMI IV. REGIS.

****

Cap. lxxxii.

An Act for making a Railway from *Merthyr Tydfil* to *Cardiff,* to be called "The *Taff Vale* Railway," with Branches. [21st *June* 1836.]

WHEREAS the making a Railway from *Merthyr Tydfil* to *Cardiff,* with a Branch therefrom, to communicate with the Tramroad leading to the several Iron Works of *Pen-y-darran, Dowlais,* and *Plymouth,* and another Branch to the Collieries called *Lancaiach,* and also a Branch to communicate with the Tramroad leading to the Collieries called *Dinas,* and another Branch leading to or near *Cogan Pill* on the West Bank of the River *Ely,* all in the County of *Glamorgan,* would be of great public Convenience by opening an additional, certain, and expeditious Means of Conveyance to the Sea for the extensive Mineral and other Produce of the Places and Works above mentioned, also for the Carriage to the said Works from the Port of *Cardiff* of Iron Ore and other Mineral Produce used in the Fabrication of Iron, and for the Conveyance of Passengers and Goods to and from the said Towns of *Merthyr Tydfil* and *Cardiff,* and the several intermediate and adjacent Towns and Districts: And whereas the several Persons herein-after named are willing at their own Expense to carry into execution the before-mentioned Undertaking; but the same cannot be effected without the Authority of Parliament: May it therefore please Your Majesty that it may be enacted; and be it enacted by the King's most Excellent Majesty, by and with the [*Local.*]   87 D   Advice

Canal that the Marquess of Bute proposed to construct in the Parish of St Mary, and the original passenger service consisted of two trains each way daily (including Sundays).

The company's first coat of arms consisted of the Prince of Wales feathers and the motto 'Ich Dien', circled with the words 'Taff Vale Railway Company'; this was later replaced with the motto 'Cymru A Fu A Chymru A Fydd', which translates into 'Wales Hath Been and Wales Shall Be'.

At Cardiff, arrangements were made with the Marquess of Bute to use a dock – he had obtained powers to build one in 1830, but they were not exercised until the railway was built. This was the 'Ship Canal' in the Parish of St Mary, afterwards called the Bute West Dock. Lord Bute welcomed the traffic the TVR would bring, but the railway also put forward a scheme for a Cogan Pill branch, much to the chagrin of Lord Bute, which would

lead to competition with his own dock. Negotiations resulted in the TVR abandoning the Cogan Pill line, in return for a long expensive lease of part of the Bute West Dock, where the TVR erected shipping devices, coal staithes and rail access to them.

In photographs and words these books show a way of life at which the older generation will nod approvingly, as they recall scenes associated with their youth – mine included – while younger people and historians will be absorbed by these accounts. Some scenes have changed a great deal due to industrial and housing developments, while nature has taken back what once was hers, changing it beyond recognition.

The modern enthusiast and railway historian owes a great debt to the photographers of years gone by, who recorded the magic of a system that changed the world.

A glass-plate photograph of Taff Vale Railway 'A' Class 0-6-2T No 132 at Brandy Bridge Junction, Merthyr. Built by the Vulcan Foundry in 1916, works number 3183, it is seen here in 1922, the last year of the TVR's independent existence. It was reboilered by the GWR with a taper boiler in 1929, renumbered 366, and withdrawn in 1955. *LCGB, Ken Nunn Collection*

INTRODUCTION

I have compiled this work as a pictorial tribute to the men and women who worked on this, the first Welsh railway, covering some of the scenes and occurrences of a daily yet much varied routine. During the 1960s many stations and halts – or 'platforms' as the were originally called – were closed, together with the branches they served, then came the 1970s, and those surviving skilfully decorated stone buildings, in all of their grand and ornate splendour, were reduced to 'bus stop' status. But by the 1990s other changes had taken place: British Rail and the local councils combined their efforts to bring back a railway service to communities that had gone without for many years, and it was finally recognised that railway services to the newly built housing estates, as well as the older-established townships, especially those in the Cynon Valley, had a need for these halts that was as great now as when the 'Taffy' first arrived.

In August 1991 the 150th Anniversary of the Taff Vale Railway was celebrated, and it was a tremendous occasion. Not only was steam back for the first time in many years, but in every valley crowds turned out in their thousands to celebrate – old-timers that had worked all their lives on these lines, their families and grandchildren. Young and old, we all shared the same feeling of nostalgia, for it had gripped us all.

Today, on the remaining Taff Vale lines, almost all of the once extensive sidings have gone, together with the coal mines that used them. The gradual disappearance of those collieries, following an almost obscene haste to close them, has opened up vast areas of land, much needed for private housing development; even the docklands and the docks themselves could not escape these modern-day changes.

Apart from the main line to Merthyr, the Taff Vale Railway owned 23 branches, covering a distance of 124 miles and 42 chains, and they are listed below in alphabetical order:

Aberdare Branch	Along the valley of the Cynon river, Abercynon to Bwllfa Dare, total 10½ miles
Aberthaw Branch	From Cowbridge to Aberthaw, total 6½ miles
Cadoxton Branch	From Penarth to Biglis Junction, total 4½ miles
Cowbridge Branch	From Llantrisant to Cowbridge, total 5¾ miles
Cwmbach Branch	Near Abercwmboi in the Aberdare Valley, total ½ mile
Dowlais Pits Branch	Between Stormstown and Abercynon, total ½ mile
East Branch	Along east side of Bute West Dock, total ¾ mile
Eirw, or Aerw, Branch	From Hafod to Cymmer, in the Rhondda Valley, total ¾ mile
Llancaiach Branch	From Stormstown to Nelson & Llancaiach, to connect with GWR at junction there, total 3¼ miles
Llandaff Loop	Connecting line between Penarth Branch and main line at Llandaff, total 29 chains
Llantrisant Branch	From Treforest to Llantrisant, where it formed junction with GWR, total 5¼ miles
Llantrisant Common Branch	From Cross Inn to junction with GWR in Ely Valley near Coedely, total 2½ miles
Llantrisant No 1 Branch	From Cross Inn to Waterhall Junction near Llandaff, total 7 miles
Penarth Branch	From Radyr to Penarth Dock and Penarth Town, total 7 miles

Penarth Harbour Branch	From Grangetown, Cardiff, to Penarth Harbour, total 1½ miles
Pont Shon Norton Branch and Cilfynydd Loop	Along eastern side of Taff Valley between Abercynon and Pontypridd, total 2½ miles
Pwllyrhebog Branch	From Tonypandy to Clydach Vale, total 2 miles
Rhondda Branch	Along valley of Rhondda Fawr river from Pontypridd to Blaenrhondda, total 12½ miles
Rhondda Fach Branch	Along valley of Rhondda Fach river from Porth to Maerdy, total 6 miles
Roath Branch	From Llandaff to Roath Dock at Cardiff, total 5 miles
Treferig Branch	Along valley of Mychydd river to Glyn Colliery, total 2¾ miles
Ynysfach Branch	From Merthyr goods yard to the Cyfarthfa Ironworks, total ½ mile
Ynysybwl Branch	Along valley of Clydach river from Stormstown to parish district of Llanwonno, total 6 miles

This volume, the first of three, is concerned principally with the main line, travelling from Cardiff to Merthyr, followed by the Cardiff East Branch, running along the east side of Bute West Dock and the west side of Bute East Dock, then a chapter dealing with the staff of the Taff Vale Railway and the later Great Western Railway, and the unions that provided guidance against bad working practises, sometimes much to the annoyance of the management. Then there is a short section on the railway's viaducts and bridges of varied and impressive design, as many rivers and roads had to be crossed, and finally signal boxes, also as varied in style and design as the locations they controlled, whether surrounded by farmland or in an extensive colliery complex.

TVR timetables for July, August and September 1892. *Cardiff Libraries and Information Services*

1. THE MAIN LINE, CARDIFF TO MERTHYR

Cardiff Dock/Bute Road

Right Cardiff Dock station opened on 8 October 1840, and the handling of goods traffic was authorised on 3 November 1840. The platform bay was relocated and a footbridge provided in July 1879. The station was renamed Bute Road by the GWR on 1 July 1924, and rebuilt in 1926/27. It closed to goods traffic on 22 March 1965, but after privatisation on 26 September 1994 it was renamed Cardiff Bay by the newly formed Regional Railways, the successor to British Rail in this area.

Taken on 16 November 1988, this photograph captures the strength of character of this former TVR terminus building, the headquarters of the Chairman and Directors of the Taff Vale Railway from 1847 to 1862. Once part of the Bute Road station complex, this Grade I listed building has gone through much renovation work, turning a derelict building into a thing of beauty. This work started in 1981, paid for by donations to the Butetown Historical Railway Centre, and by 1988 it was back in use, the downstairs as an art gallery and railway museum, while upstairs was an efficiently run café, with spare rooms available for use as lecture rooms. Also by 1988 a new station canopy was erected, as can be seen in the photo, which helped to

protect some of the volunteers working to restore the locomotives acquired. These were to be part of the Wales Railway Centre, the aim being to restore rusting, almost forgotten engines to full working order, with a line connecting Bute Road with Cardiff and perhaps further, bringing back the smell and sight of steam, as well as diesels. Locomotives on site included Nos 2861, 4115, 5227, 5539, 6686, 7927, 44901, 48518, 80150 and 92245, as well as at least two industrial engines. However, these plans fell by the wayside, not because of lack of finance or enthusiasm, but because the Cardiff Bay development had plans to take over the land, and the building is now an empty shell. Luckily, with this compulsory move a new preservation society came into being. The Vale of Glamorgan Company was formed in 1994 by members of the former Butetown Historical Society,

and all the engines and rolling-stock are now stabled on this society's land opposite Barry Island station, a short distance from the late Dai Woodham's scrapyard, where the engines languished for years – perhaps out of the ashes a phoenix, or in this case a griffin, will arise. *F. T. Hornby*

Above A Class 56XX calls at Bute Road station in the 1950s. It was on this line that the preserved engines were stabled, hidden from view by a wooden fence some 10 feet height that ran along the centre of the platform; the fence is still there today, but behind it there is only derelict ground strewn with weeds. In the far background can be seen the TVR terminus building and further still the tower of the Pierhead building, the headquarters of the former Cardiff Railway. *Lens of Sutton Collection*

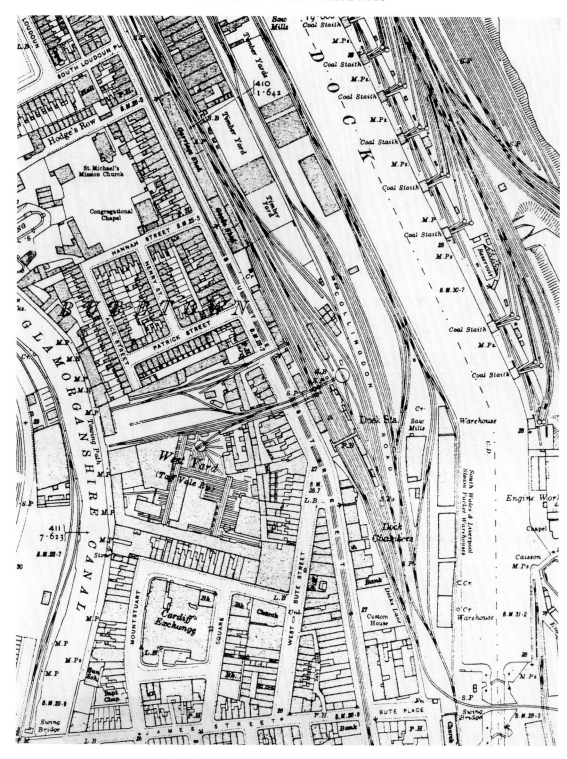

An Ordnance Survey map of 1920 showing Bute West Dock on the right, Dock (Bute Road) station in the centre, and West Yard on the opposite side of Bute Street. It demonstrates quite clearly the close vicinity of Dock station to the vast dock complex owned by Lord Bute; not only were these docks nearby, but also the buildings in Mountstuart Square (bottom of map), the financial capital of Cardiff. *Crown copyright*

Above At Bute Road station circa 1952, 14XX Class 0-4-2T No 1461 (built by the GWR in 1936 and withdrawn in 1958), with auto-coach attached, waits for passengers. This bay is still in use today. *Lens of Sutton Collection*

Right The ornate wooden waiting room built by the TVR at Bute Road station, photographed circa 1960. *J. Morgan*

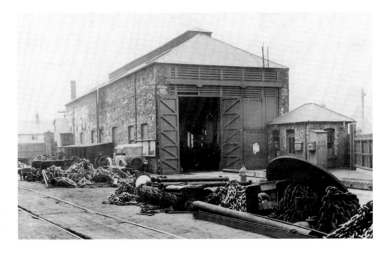

Right The former engine shed at Bute Road, seen here in 1922, in use as a store. *Roger Griffiths collection*

The Taff Vale's West Yard locomotive works were opened in October 1840, and used for the building and repair of TVR locomotives until closure in 1926.

The January 1902 edition of *The Railway Magazine* featured an interview with Mr Tom Hurry Riches, the TVR's Locomotive, Carriage & Wagon Superintendent, who described the works as follows:

'The workshops generally are rather limited in area, but the machine tools are well up to date, both in milling, turning, etc. We have a very excellent machine for testing all kinds of springs – I believe it to be the best for this purpose. This machine was built by Messrs Joshua Buckton and Co of Leeds to our specifications to do the following work, ie test all classes of bearings, drawing, buffing, and safety valve springs, either to press them home to their utmost capacity, to weigh and record the amount of deflection each spring takes under varying loads, from one pound to 12 tons; also to vibrate the spring as much as a thousand compressions per minute and to any degree up to its elastic limit. Hence every spring is tested before going out of the shop, and the buckle marked showing exactly what the spring will carry for each fraction of an inch compressed…

Our Carriage and Wagon shops are like those of our locomotive department, very limited, but we do have some good machine tools. We have for many years been steadily putting in labour-saving tools of many kinds for milling, turning, drilling, tapping, riveting,

caulking, chipping, etc, in fact pneumatic, hydraulic and other modern tools whenever possible.

The most important tools in our works today I consider are the large milling and profiling tools, some of which have vertical as well as horizontal spindles and will take cuts as much as 18 inches wide, at considerable speed. This class of machine does all our heavy work. Again, in our boiler shop we have hydraulic tools for riveting and pneumatic tools for chipping, caulking and drilling…

Regarding the tools, I may say that the milling and turning machines have been constructed by Messrs Muir & Hetherington, Sharp & Stewart, Smith & Coventry. Our hydraulic plant has been laid down by Fielding & Platt, and the pneumatic hammers, drills, etc, have been supplied by the United States Pneumatic Tool Company, also by Messrs Taite, Howard & Company.'

When asked of his views as to the manner in which British locomotives will be developed in the future, he replied:

'The development will consist in the production of more powerful engines generally, and for express passenger engines capable of travelling at a higher average speed. I think that the high-speed engine of the future must be capable of transmitting its effect to several axles in the train so as to utilise the adhesion of the whole train for

On the West Yard exit turntable on 11 August 1924 is No 488, formerly No 176, an 'M1' rebuild of the 'M' Class, built by Kitson & Co in 1891, works number 3373. Behind is No 1184, originally TVR Class 'I' No 286, built in 1884, works number 173. *LCGB, Ken Nunn Collection*

tractive purposes, and therefore I think electric power will come, but it should be generated by the locomotive, or in other words the train will carry a steam engine for the purpose of generating electric power for the haulage of the train.'

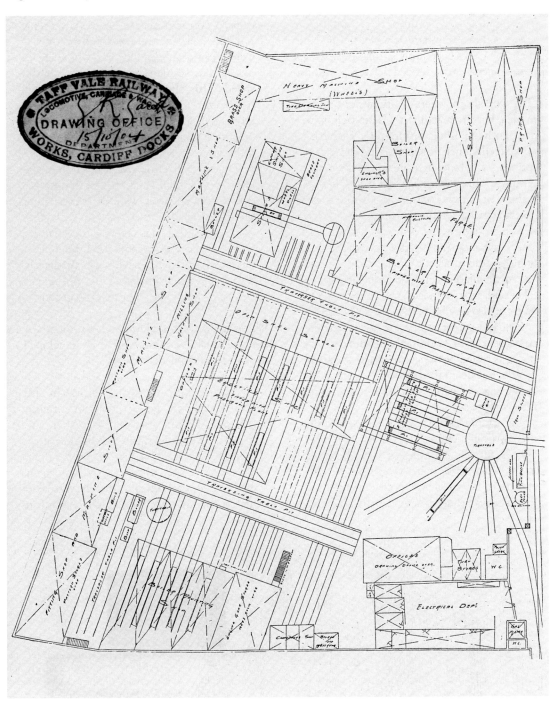

Ground plan of the West Yard works, Cardiff, from the January 1902 edition of *The Railway Magazine*.

Inset Hand stamp used by the Drawing Office at West Yard Locomotive, Carriage & Wagon Works, dated 15 October 1904. *Associated British Ports*

Above This photograph shows one of the West Yard turntables in use, with engine No 481, one of the TVR's 'M' Class originally numbered 86. It was built by the Kitson Company in 1891, under works number 3205, and was photographed on 6 August 1926. The works closed 22 days later. *National Railway Museum, York/Science Museum, London*

Below The second view of the works on the same day, but from a different angle, shows part of the traverser platform nearest the camera. *National Railway Museum, York/Science Museum, London*

Crockherbtown/ Queen Street

Top Cardiff Queen Street station opened to all traffic on 8 October 1840, and originally known as Cardiff TVR Station, Crockherbtown. Use of the original up platform ceased on 19 April 1886, after which all trains used the down platform, which had come into use on 22 May 1882; this arrangement lasted until 12 September 1887, when the reconstructed and renamed Queen Street station opened on the same site. The station was reconstructed again in 1907. The handling of goods traffic ceased on 1 April 1925, it was rebuilt again by British Rail in 1973, and is still in use for passenger services.

This photograph captures a busy scene of yesteryear very nicely, showing the entrance to Cardiff Crockherbtown station circa 1886 before the following year's rebuilding. The camera is looking towards what later became Station Terrace; around the corner on the left is the station yard, while the pony and trap wait patiently for a fare. Judging by the wheel marks on the rough ground, the TVR Directors had no thoughts of laying a cobbled surface. *Cardiff Libraries and Information Services*

Middle These former Taff Vale Railway offices were built in 1860 at the junction of Queen Street and Newport Road (see map overleaf). The photograph, taken circa 1970, gives a good view of the clock tower and the ornate workmanship of the Victorian period. The offices were demolished in 1973. *Cardiff Libraries and Information Services*

Bottom At the north end of platform 1 on 18 May 1970 the rear of the TVR offices can be seen – part of the bell tower is clearly visible. Just out of sight to the right is the bridge over Newport Road and the line towards Crockherbtown Junction, where TVR trains went left towards the Cynon, Rhondda and Taff valleys, while the Cardiff and Rhymney joint line diverged to the right. *J. Morgan*

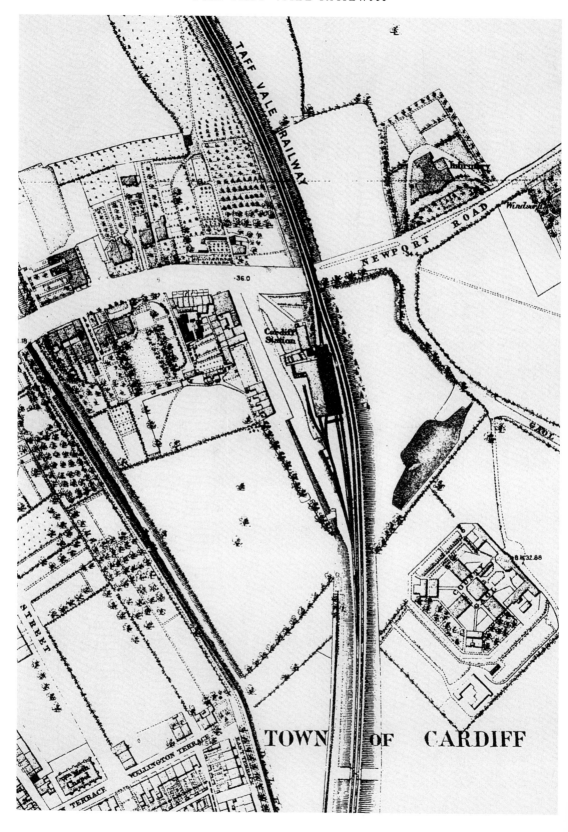

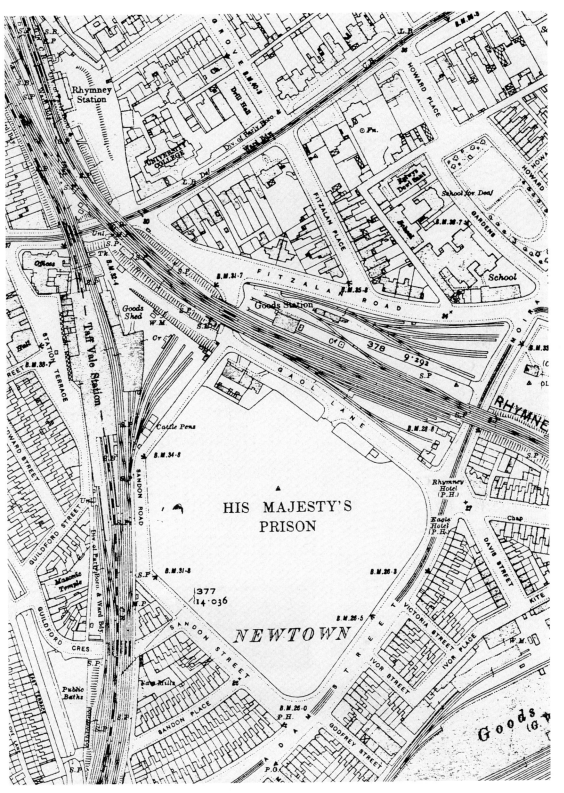

The development of the Queen Street station site, shown on Ordnance Survey maps of 1851 (*left*) and 1920. *Crown copyright*

Left This is the 1887 station, almost complete, with the down platform, built in 1882, on the right. On the left can be seen some of the original station, now part of the up platform. Shortly after this photo was taken, the buildings of 1882 were demolished to make way for the up and down mineral lines leading to the nearby docks of Lord Bute. *C. W. Harris*

Below left The new partly finished Queen Street station is seen circa 1887, showing the 1882 to 1885 layout. The building on the right is part of the 1882 construction, the original 1840s platform is now the up platform (left), and that on the right, with its long overall roof, now acts as the down platform. In 1892 the goods agent here was Mr A. Richards, by 1903 it was Mr W. W. Ash, and by 1913 Mr H. Thomas. In 1892 the Station Master was Mr C. Leyshon, then Mr Gatheridge from at least 1903 to 1913. *C. W. Harris*

Top TVR engine No 404 is seen at Queen Street station in 1922. An 'A' Class engine, built by Messrs Hawthorne Leslie in 1920, works number 3405, it was renumbered by the GWR as No 390, reboilered with a taper boiler in 1928, and withdrawn in 1957. *LCGB, Ken Nunn Collection*

Middle GWR engine No 1420 heads north past Queen Street South signal box, displaying the 'C Auto 1' target, on 5 May 1951. *R. M. Casserley*

Bottom A DMU for Bute Road stands in the bay platform (left) at Queen Street alongside the 13.20 service to Treherbert, which has arrived from Merthyr on 18 May 1970. *J. Morgan*

G.W.R. IMPROVEMENTS AT CARDIFF.

Extensive improvements are being made at the Taff Vale Station, Cardiff, preparatory to linking up with the Rhymney line. Two subways are under construction at the east side of the station.—(*South Wales Weekly News*).

Above This photograph appeared in the *Cardiff Times* of 5 September 1925, and shows the improvements being made by the GWR to link up the former TVR and Rhymney lines. The caption reads 'Extensive improvements are being made at the Taff Vale Station, Cardiff, preparatory to linking up with the Rhymney line. Two subways are under construction at the east side of the station.' This track alignment work was completed in 1928. *Cardiff Libraries and Information Services*

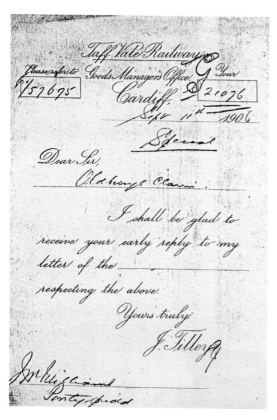

THEATRE ROYAL, CARDIFF.

:o:

Lessee and Manager - - Mr Edward Fletcher.
Acting Manager - - - - Mr John Sheridan.

:o:

GRAND PRODUCTION ON A SCALE OF UN-
RIVALLED MAGNIFICENCE

Of Mr Edward Fletcher's Fourth Christmas
Pantomime

YE QUEEN OF HEARTS,

Her Wonderful Tarts and ye Knave who stole
them.

SPECIAL SELECTED COMPANY OF ARTISTES:
MISS JULIA BALLEN,
Mr Alberto and Miss Haler in their astounding
SOMERSAULT DANCE.

PROCESSION OF THE KINGS AND QUEENS
OF ENGLAND,

From William the First to Queen Victoria.
Grand Transformation " Birth of the Rose."
New Comic Harlequinade invented by the
CLOWN—THE FAMOUS JOLLY LITTLE LEWIS

SPECIAL PANTOMIME TRAIN ARRANGEMENTS.

MR. FLETCHER has much pleasure in an-
nouncing that he has arranged with the RAIL-
WAY COMPANIES to run a service of SPECIAL
TRAINS, enabling visitors from the district to
witness this magnificent pantomime.

TAFF VALE RAILWAY.

To Pontypridd. Treherbert, Ferndale, &c., on
THURSDAY NIGHTS, Jan. 1st and 22nd. To
Pontypridd, Aberdare, &c., THURSDAY, Jan
8th and 29th. To Pontypridd, Merthyr, &c., Jan
15th and Feb. 5th. Leaving Cardiff at 11.10 p.m.

RHYMNEY RAILWAY.

To Rhymney, FRIDAY, Dec. 26th, SATURDAY,
Dec. 27th, THURSDAY, Jan. 8th. To Dowlais.
THURSDAY, Jan. 1st, leaving Cardiff at 11.15
p.m.

GREAT WESTERN RAILWAY.

To Swansea, THURSDAY, Jan. 1st, 1885, leaving
Cardiff at 11 p.m.

All the above Trains stop at intermediate
Stations.

Special Reduced Fares to persons purchasing
tickets for the Theatre. Ticket-holders admitted
by early doors without extra charge. Doors open
7; commence at 7.15. Stage door and St. Mary
Street Entrance open at 6.15; Sixpence extra.
Plans as usual Box plan at Messrs. Thompson
and Shackell's, Crockherbtown.

DAY PERFORMANCES.

FRIDAY, Dec. 26th (Boxing Day), SATURDAY,
Dec. 27th, and every day till further notice, at
Two o'clock. Doors open at Half-past one.

Above 'Special Pantomime Train Arrangements' from the *Pontypridd Chronicle*, 6 January 1885. *Pontypridd Library*

Left A TVR memo, dated 11 September 1906. *J. Morgan collection*

Taff Vale Railway

CARDIFF, QUEEN STREET

TO

ABERAVON

R. & S. B. Via Treherbert

Taff Vale Railway.

CARDIFF, T.V.R.,

TO

Cymmer

R. & S. B.

Above TVR luggage labels. *L. D. Bryant*

SPECIAL WHISTLES. — **Main Lines.**

STATIONS AND JUNCTIONS.	TO AND FROM	WHISTLES.	REMARKS.
Cardiff Terminus ...	Platform Road	1	
	No. 1 Goods Road and Drop Pit ...	1 short and 1 crow	
	No. 2 Goods Road	2 crows	
	Up Line and Goods Road	2	
	1 & 2 Turntable Roads and Up Line...	3	
	„ „ and Drop Pit ...	2 short and 1 crow	
	„ „ and Machine Road	2 and 2 short	
	„ „ and Coal Stage ...	4 short	By Through Shunt on Passenger Road
	Coal-Stage and Drop Pit	2 short and 2 crows	
	„ and Machine	2 crows and 2 short	
	„ and Up Line	2 and 1 short	
	Up Line and Passenger Road... · ...	5 short	Through Compound Shunt
	„ and Carriage Shed	2 crows and 1	
	Machine Road	1 crow	
24			

SPECIAL WHISTLES. — **Main Lines (Con.)**

STATIONS AND JUNCTIONS.	TO AND FROM	WHISTLES.	REMARKS.
Cardiff Terminus ...	New Siding	1 crow and 1 short	
	New Siding and Down Line	1 and 1 short	
	Machine Road and Long Siding ...	1 and 2 crows	
Bute Street Points ...	Van Siding and Up Line	1 crow	
	Spillers' Siding and Down No. 2 ...	1 crow and 1 short	
East Branch ...	No. 1 Down and Back Road	1 and 1 short	
	No. 2 „ „	2 and 1 short	
	No. 3 „ „	3 and 1 short	
	No. 1 Down Line and Up Empty Road	1 crow	
	Empty Tip Road and Up Line ...	1 short and 1 crow	
	„ „ and No. 1 Empty .	1 crow and 1 short	
	Up Line and No. 1 Empty Storage ...	1 and 1 crow	
	„ and No. 2 „ ...	1 and 2 crows	
	Back Road and No. 1 Empty Storage.	2 short and 1 crow	
25			

Right TVR code of engine whistles for
'Cardiff Terminus', 22 October 1894.
T. D. Chapman

[10] CARDIFF DOCKS, CARDIFF (QUEEN ST.), CATHAYS (WOODVILLE RD) & MAINDY (NORTH ROAD). WEEKDAYS.			
Cardiff Docks, dep.	Cardiff (Queen Street), dep.	Cathays (Wdville Road) arr.	Maindy (North Road) arr.
a.m.	a.m.	a.m.	a.m.
6 50	6 54	..	..
8 40	8 44	8 47	8 50
..	..	..	..
9 1	9 5	9 7	9 10
9 22	9 27	9 30	9 35
9 50	9 55	9 58	10 1
10*10	10*14	..	..
10 42	10 46	..	..
..	..	11 3	11 6
11 0	11 4	11 6	..
p.m.	p.m.	p.m.	p.m.
12 20 P	12 25 P	12 28 P	12 30 P
12 38	12 42	12 44	12 47
12*50†R	12*54†R	..	..
1 2	..	1 9	1 12
1* 5†	1* 9†	..	..
1 30S	1 35S	1 37S	1 44S
1†30F	1†35F	1†28F	1†41F
1 57S	2 2S	2 1S	2 7S
2 18S	2 22S	2 24S	2 27S
2 50S	2 54S	..	..
..	..	..	..
3 53S	3 57S	..	..
4*25S	4*29S	..	..
5† 3S	..	5† 9S	5†12S
5* 8†S	5*12†S	..	..
5 25S	..	5 31S	5 34S
5*30S	5*34S	..	..
†5*49S	†5*53S	..	..
6 0S	6 6S	6 8S	6 11S
6 25S	6 30S	6 33S	6 36S
6*†34FS	6*†38FS	..	..
..	..	..	..
..	10 30 P	10 33 P	10 36 P

* Denotes train. Trips not so marked are run by cars.
† Conveys Workmen as well as Ordinary Passengers on Saturdays.
‡ Conveys Workmen as well as Ordinary Passengers.
F Runs through to Taff's Well.   S Not run on Saturdays.
P Through Car to Pontypridd.   R Runs through to Radyr.

MAINDY (NORTH ROAD), CATHAYS (WOODVILLE [11] ROAD), CARDIFF (QUEEN ST.) AND CARDIFF DOCKS. WEEKDAYS.			
Cathays (Wdville Road) dep.	Maindy (North Road) dep.	Cardiff [Queen Street] dep.	Cardiff Docks. arr.
a.m.	a.m.	a.m	a.m.
..	..	6§40A	6§44
7§10	..	7§14	7§18
..	..	7*31	7*35
8 25	8 28	8 32	8 36
..	..	8*38B	8*42
..	..	8*47	8*51
8 48	8 52	8 55	8 59
..	..	9° 2	9° 6
9 8	9 11	9 18	9 18
..	..	X9°28	9°32
..	..	9°36	9°40
9 34	9 38	9 43	9 47
9 59	10 4	10 8	10 12
..	..	X10 50	10 54
..	..	11*34	11°38
11 55	..	11 59	12 3
p.m.	p.m.	p.m.	p.m.
12 23	..	12 27	12 31
12 45	12 48	12 52	12 56
1 10	1 13	1 20	1 24
1 42S	1 45S	1 50S	1 54S
..	..	2* 4	2* 8
2 5S	2 8S	..	2 15S
..	..	2*17	2*21
2 25S	2 28S	2 32S	2 36S
..	..	A2 41S	2 45S
..	..	X3 30S	3 34S
5 10S	5 14S	5 18S	5 22S
..	..	5*58S	6* 2S
..	..	6*32S	6*36S

* Denotes train. Trips not so marked are run by cars.
§ Conveys Ordinary Passengers and Workmen
A Runs through from Pontypridd.
B Runs through from Taff's Well.
S Not run on Saturdays.
X All Down Trains and Cars for Cardiff Docks leave Cardiff Queen St. from the Down Platform except those marked X which leave from the Up Platform.

Cathays

Left TVR timetable of railmotors and trains, 2 February 1920. The passenger service between Cardiff Bute Road and Maindy North Road Halt was inaugurated on 2 July 1906, and lasted until 15 September 1958, when it was withdrawn. *D. K. Jones collection*

Below left An aerial photograph of the TVR's extended coal sidings at Cathays circa 1945, beyond the National Museum, Cardiff. In view are coal wagons en route to Cardiff Docks. This is now the site of the present-day Cathays station. *Powell Duffryn Wagon Company*

Below An Ordnance Survey map of 1920, showing Cathays Yard and the Carriage and Engine Sheds. Just out of sight, top left, is Maindy Halt, and also off the map at bottom right is the location of Woodville Halt. *Crown copyright*

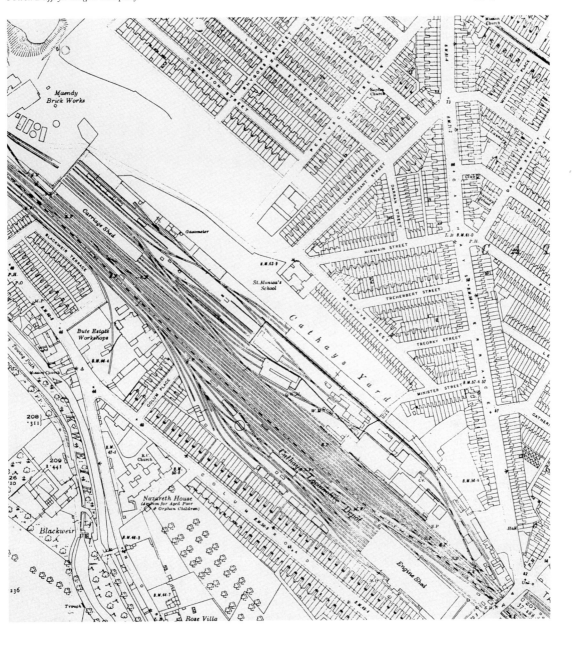

Above Cathays Woodville Road Platform was opened on 2 July 1906, and renamed Cathays Woodville Road Halt by the GWR on 10 July 1922. British Railways renamed it Woodville Road Halt on 15 September 1952, the word Cathays being dropped, and it eventually closed for passenger services on 15 September 1958. The Halt was served by local up services only; passengers who wanted to go to Cardiff travelled up to Maindy Halt, where the service then crossed over on to the down side for the return to Cardiff. Here an up valleys passenger train passes circa 1922, with the Exchange Sidings in the background, though half hidden by the smoke. *LCGB, Ken Nunn Collection*

Below Cathays Carriage and Wagon Works opened in 1845 for the construction and repair of carriages. This work ceased in 1905, and it then concentrated on wagon repairs only, finally closing in 1993. The engine shed at Cathays opened in 1884, and was replaced in about 1937/38 by a GWR-designed shed, which closed on 30 November 1957. Today private housing and buildings owned by Cardiff University cover the area. A splendid stable of engines range across the front of the TVR shed circa 1921. *R. Griffiths collection*

Above This broader view, taken on 25 August 1935, again shows the TVR stone-built ten-road shed. The GWR built a new coaling stage here in 1931. *R. Griffiths collection*

Right Outside the shed on 1 May 1927 is TVR 4-4-2T No 175, seen here with its GWR number 1304; it was built in the Vulcan Foundry in 1891 as works number 1314. Behind it is No 320, formerly TVR 'O4' Class No 116, built by the Beyer Peacock Company, works number 5390, in 1910. *R. M. Casserley*

Right In Cathays yard is No 320 again. This former TVR '04' Class loco was photographed on 1 May 1927. *R. M. Casserley*

Above Another former TVR engine, 'A' Class' 0-6-2T No 125, is seen here alongside Cathays engine shed as GWR No 360, minus its trailing wheels. Built by the Vulcan Foundry in July 1916 as works number 3178 and reboilered with a taper boiler in 1929, it was photographed on 29 June 1952 and withdrawn from service in 1955. Also seen is the brick cladding that covered the former TVR stonework, part of the GWR redesign programme. *F. T. Hornby*

Left Another former TVR 'A' Class engine, No 45, is seen here circa 1953 with its GWR number 346. Built in 1915 by the North British Locomotive Company under works number 21157, it was reboilered by the GWR in 1928 with a taper boiler, and was withdrawn from service in 1955. Just visible behind is No 376, the former TVR No 149, built in 1920 by Hawthorn Leslie as works number 3397. This was also rebuilt by the GWR with a taper boiler in 1932, and withdrawn in 1957. *G. W. Sharpe*

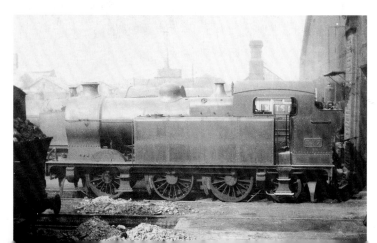

Left Outside the shed on 1 May 1927 is No 387, originally TVR No 401, also built by Hawthorn Leslie in 1920 and given works number 3402. Rebuilt with a taper boiler in 1928, this photograph shows it in its original form. It was withdrawn in 1956. *R. M. Casserley*

Inside Cathays engine repair shop on 6 May 1951 are GWR engines No 5635 (left), No 6416 (centre) and former TVR engine, GWR number 371. The latter is another 'A' Class engine, formerly No 136, built by Nasmyth Wilson in 1919 under works number 1271. In 1930 it was rebuilt by the GWR with a taper boiler, and withdrawn from service in 1955, No 5635 was built in 1925 and withdrawn in 1964, while No 6416 was built in 1934 and withdrawn in 1963. *R. M. Casserley*

No 305, formerly TVR 'A' Class No 413, was built at the Hawthorn Leslie works in 1920 under works number 3414, reboiled by the GWR in 1927 with a taper boiler, and withdrawn from service in 1957. It is surrounded by an assortment of parts in the repair shop on 6 May 1951. *R. M. Casserley*

Inside Cathays shed on 6 May 1951 are, from left to right, Nos 390, 1420 and 3698 – note the ventilation arrangements. No 390 was built in 1920 by Hawthorn Leslie, order number 3405, and was numbered by the TVR as 404; reboiled in 1928 by the GWR with a taper boiler, it was withdrawn from service in 1957. The other two engines are 'pure' GWR: No 1420 was built in 1933 and withdrawn in 1964, and No 3698 was built in 1941 and withdrawn in 1964. *R. M. Casserley*

On Monday, the workmen in the employ of the Taff Vale Railway Company, at the Cathays Yard, Cardiff, together with their wives, sweethearts, and children, numbering about 1,700, had their annual excursion, starting from Cardiff between 8 and 9. Penydarren Park was the scene of their day's festivities, returning about half-past seven.

'Epitome of news', *Pontypridd Chronicle*, 10 September 1881. *Pontypridd Library*

Cardiff Libraries and Information Services

This article, which appeared in the *Cardiff & Merthyr Guardian* of 17 July 1858, is very interesting. It gives not only the Rules and Regulations of the company regarding tenders, but also the vigorous rules that governed the strengths of the many components used in the construction of many items that were in daily use by the Taff Vale Railway Company. For example:

NAVES

The naves to be of the best toughened cast iron, twelve inches in diameter and seven inches wide, to be bored to a size to fit the wheels, so as to require powerful hydraulic pressure to force the wheels onto the axles.

AXLE BOXES

The axle boxes are to be of cast iron, with proper bearing brasses, ample space for grease, and proper grease covers, acting with springs and straps complete.

AXLE GUARDS

Every wagon, truck, and other vehicle must have proper axle guards well fitted to the boxes, with angle stays and guard rods complete.

SPRINGS

The springs to be not less than three feet long for all vehicles under twelve feet in length, and not less than three feet six inches long for all wagons, trucks, or other vehicles measuring in length twelve feet and upwards, the springs to consist of not less than twelve plates, to be sufficiently strong to support the superincumbent weight, with an average deflection of three inches.

The camber of the springs with the empty vehicle to be six inches, and the distance from the surface of the rails to the centre of buffers or soles to be three feet one inch.

DRAW BARS AND COUPLINGS

Every vehicle to be fitted with proper draw springs, one at each end, the draw bars and springs attached must be sufficiently strong, with not less than two inches spring, the centre coupling must be of three links and one shackle, the links are to be not less than one inch in diameter.

Every vehicle must have four safety or side couplings, with proper hooks, the links to be not less than seven eights of an inch in diameter, and each side coupling to be placed at a distance of six inches from the centre coupling, the shackles to be made to fit the drawbar, the holes in the drawbar to be one inch and three eights in diameter, the coupling pins to be one and a quarter inch in diameter, and not less than eight inches long, the couplings to be of such length as to leave a space between the buffers of not less than four inches, nor more than six inches, the side couplings must be two inches longer than the centre couplings, the whole of the couplings, including the drawbar, to be made from the best faggotted iron.

BRAKES

Every vehicle to be provided with a good and efficient brake, applied in such manner as to act upon two wheels simultaneously, to be fitted with a proper brake guard, to effectually confine the lever and to prevent the same from falling to the ground, with proper catches and pins to support the same, the brake levers to be placed at the tailboard end of the vehicle, and upon the right-hand side of the same, looking into the vehicle.

UNDER FRAMING

The under framing to be all of British Oak timber, or wrought iron of such quality, scantling, and sectional area as shall be approved of by the company's general superintendent.

BUFFERS

Every truck or other vehicle (not being a coal wagon) under twelve feet in length of body, must be furnished with approved spring buffers at each end, of not less than twelve inches in diameter. Coal wagons under twelve feet length of body must be furnished with approved spring buffers placed at the tailboard end, of not less than ten inches in diameter, and with not less than four inch stroke. At the opposite end the buffer blocks are to be secured to the sole pieces and bound by strong iron hoops.

BOARDING

Every vehicle to be made and well maintained with good red pine boarding.

Every vehicle to be properly painted. Every vehicle must be carefully examined, and well greased at the end of each journey. Every article must have the owner's name and tare plate in place, both sides thereof.

By order of the Board of Directors
Edward Kenway, Secretary

A prefabricated crossover has been partly assembled in the Permanent Way Yard at Cathays Works circa 1907. The PW office can be seen behind the crossover, while over to the left of the yard crane is an assembly of Great Western colliery wagons. *J. Dore-Dennis collection*

Brush diesel-electric No D1901 passes Cathays Yard on 1 November 1968, working a Deep Navigation Colliery to Aberthaw Power Station service with 'merry-go-round' hoppers. This engine was allocated to Barry MPD, and later became Class 47 No 47225. On the left are the derelict and abandoned remains of the engine shed. *J. Morgan*

SPECIAL WHISTLES. Main Lines (Con.)

STATIONS AND JUNCTIONS.	TO AND FROM	WHISTLES.	REMARKS.
Roath Line Junction ...	Down Branch Line and Blind End ...	1 crow and 1 short	Down trains on No. 2 if all Cardiff traffic sound destination Whistle. If to put off at Roath Line, must sound Standard Whistle for Junction.
	" " and Full Sidings...	3 short	
Llandaff Station ...	Up " and Empty " ...	4 short	
	No. 2 Up and Lower Shunt to Goods	4 short	
	No. 2 Up and Upper "	1 crow	
Penarth Junction ...	No. 2 Up and Empty Sidings...	2, 1 crow and 1 short	
	No. 1 Down & Cardiff Traffic Sidings	3 short	
	No. 2 Down and " "	4 short	
	Up Branch and " "	1 crow	
	" and Shunting "	2 crows	
	Shed Road and Empty "	2 short	
	Radyr Stores ...	1 crow and 3 short	

SUPPLEMENTARY LIST OF ENGINE WHISTLES brought into force in connection with Penarth Junction Alterations.

STATIONS AND JUNCTIONS.	TO AND FROM	WHISTLES.	REMARKS.
Penarth Junction ...	Loco. Yard and Up Shunting Siding	2 short and 1 crow	This cancels Notice No. 2,015, dated April 22nd, 1898. All other Engine Whistles will remain unaltered.
	Nos. 1, 2, or 3 Up Sidings and Up Passenger Line	1 short, 1 crow and 1 short	
	Nos. 1, 2, or 3 Up Sidings and Up Mineral Line	1 short, 1 crow and 2 short	
	Nos. 1, 2, or 3 Up Sidings and Up Shunting Siding	1 long and 3 short	
	Down Branch Line and Up Passenger Line	1 long, 2 crows and 1 short	
	Down Branch Sidings and Up Passenger Line	1 long, 2 crows and 2 short	
	No. 4 Up Siding and Up Mineral Line	4 short and 2 long	
	No. 4 Up Siding and Up Shunting Siding	5 short	
	No. 4 Up Siding and No. 1 Traffic Siding	5 short and 1 crow	
	Nos. 5, 6, 7, or 8 Up Sidings and No. 1 Traffic Siding	1 crow and 2 short	

SPECIAL WHISTLES. Main Lines (Con.)

STATIONS AND JUNCTIONS.	TO AND FROM	WHISTLES.	REMARKS.
Crockherbtown Lower Junction ...	West Dock interchange Sidings ...	3 crows and 1	After obtaining the Signal will give three short if ordered to pick up at Cathays or Empty Storage
	R.R. and High Level ...	2	
	Passing Gaol Lane Cabin Up...	2	
	Up and Down Lines ...	1	
Crockherbtown Upper Junction ...	Steam Shed and No. 1 ...	1 crow	
	No. 2 Up and Storage Sidings	1 and 3 short	
	" and No. 1 Empty Storage...	2 and 3 short	
Maindy Bridge ...	No. 1 Down and Crown Siding	1 and 3 short	
	No. 2 " " "	2 and 3 short	
	No. 2 Up " "	4 short	
	Cathays Yard " "	1 crow and 3 short	
	Shed Road and No. 1 Up ...	2 crows and 1 short	
	No. 1 Up and Star Fuel ...	5 short	

SPECIAL WHISTLES. Main Lines (Con.)

STATIONS AND JUNCTIONS.	TO AND FROM	WHISTLES.	REMARKS.
Maindy Bridge ...	Empty Storage and No. 1 Up...	1 and 2 crows	
	" Lower Shunt and No. 2 Up	2 and 2 crows	
	" Top Shunt and No. 2 Up...	2 and 1 crow	
Maindy Fuel ...	Up Line and Sidings ...	1 crow	See Special Whistle, page 13. See Appendix
Roath Dock ...			
Roath Dock Storage Upper ...	Up Line and Empty Sidings ...	1 crow	
	Down Line and Full Sidings ...	2 crows	
Roath Line Junct. South ...	Up Main Line and Up Sidings ...	2 short	
	No. 1 Down Siding and Down Line	1 crow	
	All other " " ...	2 crows	
	Down Line and Empty Sidings and Coal Stage	4 short	
Roath Line Junction ...	Up Branch Line and Blind End ...	1 crow	
	Empty Sidings and "	2 crows and 1 short	
	Down Sidings and "	2 crows and 2 short	

TVR code of engine whistles for the line through Maindy and Llandaff, 22 October 1894. *T. D. Chapman*

Maindy to Radyr

Hurriedly snapped from the carriage window of a passing train on 3 June 1968, this photograph shows the disused Maindy Bridge signal box, opened in 1956 and closed on 27 June 1966. Standing disused for many years, it was destroyed by fire on 24 April 1987. *D. G. Thomas*

An up valleys train is about to pass Maindy Halt circa 1922 – it is unfortunate that much of the engine smoke is obscuring the view of Cathays Carriage Works. This halt, originally known as Maindy North Road Platform, opened in May 1907 (or possibly as early December 1906) for passenger services; it became known as Maindy North Road Halt on 10 July 1922, then simply Maindy Halt from 15 September 1952. It closed on 15 September 1958, and today no trace remains of it, or Woodville Road Halt. The sidings on the right lead off into the nearby council and water board depot. *LCGB, Ken Nunn Collection*

Another view of Maindy Halt, this time from ground level looking towards Llandaff, with a TVR engine pulling the 12.40pm down passenger service en route from Merthyr to Cardiff Queen Street. It is about to pass the original Maindy Bridge signal box, opened by the TVR in 1890 and replaced by a British Railways design in 1956. The engine in this slightly blurred view is one of the 'A' Class, built at the Vulcan Foundry in 1921 as works number 3492, and given the TVR number 75. It was renumbered by the GWR to 347, received a taper boiler in 1927, and was withdrawn in 1956; it is seen here in its original condition circa 1922. *LCGB, Ken Nunn Collection*

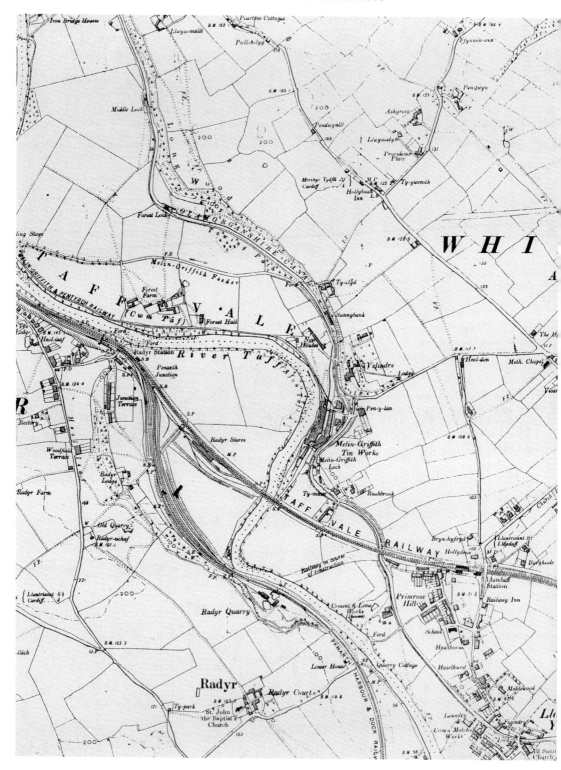

This Ordnance Survey map of 1901 shows the TVR's proposed Llandaff Loop Line, which was then under construction (just below the words 'TAFF VALE' on the main line), while the private Melin Griffith Tin Works line can be clearly seen in the centre of the map. *Crown copyright*

Right From the *Pontypridd Observer*, 2 April 1904.
Pontypridd Library

Above Llandaff station was opened for passenger and goods services on 8 October 1840, and this photograph, taken from street level on 30 April 1968, shows the elevated booking office situated next to the Parade. Originally passengers could only reach the down platform by using the footbridge at the side. The station is still in use for passenger services. *D. G .Thomas*

WHY STOP AT LLANDAFF?

There is now an excellent service of trains on the Taff Vale Railway, but there is one more improvement that travellers between Pontypridd and Cardiff would much appreciate. Even the expresses stop at Llandaff in order that the tickets might be collected, and this usually means a delay of about five minutes. Could not the management arrange for a few trains to run right through from Pontypridd to Cardiff without stopping? The tickets could be collected at Pontypridd station, and if these particular trains started at the exact minute through travellers would soon favour them. Is there any reason why we should not be able to get to Cardiff from Pontypridd in fifteen minutes? The manager of the Taff Vale Railway has given us plenty of trains, will he go a step further and give us this improvement as well?

Right This is Llandaff station as seen from the up platform looking towards Cathays circa 1960. The up platform has a mixture of buildings, much varied in design and shape – next to the house is the waiting room, then the parcels office – while the down platform has a long range of buildings beneath a large canopy. A wooden nameboard near the footbridge was inscribed 'Llandaff for Whitchurch', the station name introduced by the TVR on 1 December 1896. The roof of the elevated booking office can be seen on the left, and in the distance can be glimpsed the bridge that carries Station Road over the line; a plaque attached to this bridge stated 'F. Finch Company Limited, Engineers and Ironfounders, Chepstow, 1903'. *Lens of Sutton Collection*

Right A down passenger train leaves Llandaff station en route to Cardiff circa 1922. TVR 'A' Class engine No 401, built by Hawthorn Leslie in 1920, works number 3402, was given the number 387 by the GWR; it was reboilered with a taper boiler in 1928, and withdrawn by British Railways in 1956. In the background can be seen the rear of the high-level booking office. To the right is a three-plank engineering wagon carrying spoil; the letters 'N' and 'B', with an 'E' in a circle between them, can be clearly seen on the wooden sides. *LCGB, Ken Nunn Collection*

Just north of Llandaff station was Llandaff Loop Junction signal box, opened in 1900, closed by Regional Railways in May 1998 and demolished by Railtrack on 5 June 1998; it is seen here in November 1985. The Llandaff Loop Line diverges to the left, towards the River Taff, to join the TVR's Penarth branch; prior to crossing the river this short spur had also to cross the former Glamorgan Canal (see the map on page 34). *Author*

Radyr Yard signal box is seen here in a disused state, looking towards Radyr station, photographed from the carriage of a down train on 3 June 1968. *D. G. Thomas*

On 3 March 1985 Class 37 No 37213, one of the workhorses of the valley lines, pulls a heavy load of steel-sided coal wagons destined for the valleys past Radyr Junction signal box, designed by British Railways and opened on 4 June 1961; this was another box closed by Regional Railways, and demolished by Railtrack in August 1998. Traffic of this type usually came from Bedwas or Onllwyn, small coal en route to the Nantgarw Coke Works. *B. Phillips*

Top Radyr station opened in June 1863. Former Rhymney Railway 'R' Class No 41 hauls a mixed rake of goods vans past Radyr Junction on 5 May 1961, heading up the valley and showing the 'Y15' target. Formerly No 45, the engine was built by Beyer Peacock in 1921 under works number 6101, and even in GWR ownership it retained its original parallel boiler, being withdrawn from service in 1956. It is on a Radyr Junction to Treherbert Junction service, and through the smoke can be seen the earlier TVR Radyr Junction signal box. The sidings on the right are for stabling wagons and diesel locomotives, and beside them is the former TVR booking office in the dark red brick edged with yellow engineering stone much favoured by the railways in South Wales. Behind it is the original TVR-constructed underpass to allow pedestrians to reach the down platform; in later years this underpass became part of Station Road. In 1983 the up sidings were lifted and the area converted into a park-and-ride facility. The station closed to the handling of goods traffic on 6 January 1964, but is still in use for passenger services. *R. M. Casserley*

Middle On the down platform can be seen the TVR timber-clad waiting room, the zig-zag pattern making it quite an attractive little building, certainly a much better waiting area than the 'bus stop' shelters in use today; beside it the wooden fence borders the railway path leading to and from the underpass. The bench is of pure GWR design, while on the near side of the tracks can be seen a lamp post of the much-used 'swan neck' design, and just in sight on the right is part of the booking office. The engine, 61XX Class No 6116, was built in the GWR shops at Swindon in 1931, and was withdrawn from service in 1965; it is seen here hauling a rake of British Railways all-steel 16-ton mineral wagons on 23 September 1964. *B. J. Ashworth*

Bottom This view looking north up the valley towards Pentyrch and Taffs Well circa 1912 gives a panoramic view of the station. The land dips down to the River Taff on the right, and rises on the left, so many tons of earth must have been excavated to level the site. Next to the waiting room on the right two men wait patiently in front of the enamel Sunlight Soap advert, while beside the booking office on the left a one-legged man rests on his crutches; this was not an uncommon sight in an area of busy railway traffic, and often reflected the poor safety standards of the collieries. From right to left, the tracks are the up and down main lines, then the up and down relief lines, then the stabling sidings. *Lens of Sutton Collection*

Left Looking south towards Llandaff on 5 May 1951, the original TVR-designed footbridge at Radyr can be seen, one part linking the up and down platforms and the other allowing pedestrians to cross the extensive sidings on the right. These sidings were lifted in 1983, and in approximately the area where the footbridge steps start is where a British Rail-designed booking office was placed. The down-side waiting room is again noticeable at the far end of the up platform, and opposite on the right can be seen the TVR booking office. *R. M. Casserley*

Above 56XX Class No 5648 arrives at Radyr station with the 4.28pm passenger service from Cardiff Bute Road to Merthyr. This former GWR engine was built in 1925 at Swindon and withdrawn in 1964, some two years after this photograph was taken in May 1962; by now the TVR footbridge has gone, although the up and down platforms were connected again by a British Rail-designed footbridge in November 1983. *G. Pearce*

BREAKDOWN OF A TAFF VALE PASSENGER TRAIN.

The second down passenger train from Merthyr on Saturday came to a breakdown at Radyr. For some reason the engine "slowed up" up considerably between Walnut Tree Junction and Radyr, and it appears there was not sufficient steam to start again. A mineral engine was put in front, and, as the vacuum break would not act, the train was kept waiting some time, and ultimately, the power of the mineral engine had to be used to pull the train and passenger engine, the breaks being on during the greater part, if not the whole, of the journey to Cardiff. There, however, the engine and break were declared to have got all right.

Left From the *Pontypridd Chronicle*, 6 February 1885. *Pontypridd Library*

Top The picturesque Castell Coch looks down on a former GWR engine hauling a rake of mineral wagons, of all-steel construction, at Pentyrch Crossing. The train is the 12.50pm Llanbradach Colliery to Cathays Sidings mineral train, with a 'C8' target, on Saturday 8 February 1958. No 5669 was stabled at Radyr; built in 1926 at Swindon, it was withdrawn from service in September 1964, but after a period in Dai Woodham's scrapyard on Barry Island it was rescued for preservation. This area was one of the late Sid Rickard's favourite places, and having spent many a quiet hour looking down on this line myself, I fully agree with him. Behind the wagons is Pentyrch Crossing signal box, which opened in 1901 and was taken out of use on 7 October 1962, and next to it is the former Pentyrch station house. *The late S. Rickard, J and J collection*

Middle This photograph was also taken by the late Sid Rickard on the same day, and shows No 5687 pulling empty mineral wagons en route from the marshalling sidings at Cardiff Docks to Ogilvie Colliery. Nearest the camera is the Melin Griffith private line, which crossed the Taff Vale metals; on the right of this photograph can be seen the loading gauge hanging above the Melin Griffith siding. This was the tin works' southern connection with the TVR; before the days of the railway, the works was a major user of the Glamorgan Canal, which ran beside it, and the line crossing here at Pentyrch was a horse-drawn tramway. The works was only a short distance from the crossing gate seen on the left, next to Pentyrch Crossing signal box. *The late S. Rickard, J and J collection*

Bottom Pentyrch station opened on 8 October 1840 for passenger services, closing entirely with the opening of Radyr station in June 1863. This is the former station house, in which the photographer lived in as a boy; perhaps the atmosphere of living so close to the line led him to photograph the varied TVR sights, some of which I have had the pleasure to reproduce in my books. For those interested in railway modelling, this is a view not often seen, photographed on 7 April 1964. *D. G. Thomas*

Taffs Well

Below This second Taffs Well station has carried several names. First the Rhymney Railway opened its station, Walnut Tree Bridge, on 31 March 1858 at the bottom of the 'big hill', a local term for that company's Walnut Tree Branch, which opened to mineral traffic on 25 February 1858 and went from Aber Junction via Penrhos to Walnut Tree Bridge and a junction with the Taff Vale metals, just south of Taffs Well village. The TVR hoped to make this a joint station, but this did not happen, so on 22 June 1863 it opened its own Walnut Tree Junction station. On 1 June 1886 the name was changed to Walnut Tree Bridge, and finally on 1 April 1900 it was renamed Taffs Well. The Station Master at Walnut Tree Bridge in 1892 was Mr G. James, in 1903 it was Mr R. Carpenter, and by 1913 Mr W. C. John. The station closed to goods traffic on 27 June 1966, but is still in use for passenger services. the signal box at the

Radyr end of the up platform has always been called Walnut Tree Junction box, and nearby, close to the junction with the Rhymney Railway, that company had an engine shed from 1885 to 1922, used for the stabling of the banking engine used to assist engines on the 'big hill'; long unused for railway purposes, is still in situ today.

This is Walnut Tree Junction station circa 1885, looking north towards Treforest; as can be seen, the original signal box, opened in 1879, was located on the down side, as it not only oversaw TVR traffic, but also the Rhymney Railway traffic that branched off the TVR line at this point. It can be seen that the buildings on both platforms are of wooden construction. *C. W. Harris*

Bottom Looking in the opposite direction, from the down platform, this 1904 view includes the station staff, the local vicar and, on the far right, Mr Thomas; what regiment the sergeant is from is unknown. The wooden station buildings are of an attractive design; they were later replaced by buildings made from bricks left over from the rebuilt Pontypridd station. The enamelled sign on the waiting room wall advertises Hudson's Soap, a popular product in those days. In the background is the Barry Railway's Walnut Tree viaduct. *Courtesy of the family of the late Mrs M. Griffiths, née Thomas*

Right Because of the narrowness of the valley at Taffs Well, a river, a canal, four railway companies and a private railway were all squeezed into its natural confines, and this Ordnance Survey map of 1921 shows the situation better than any amount of words. *Crown copyright*

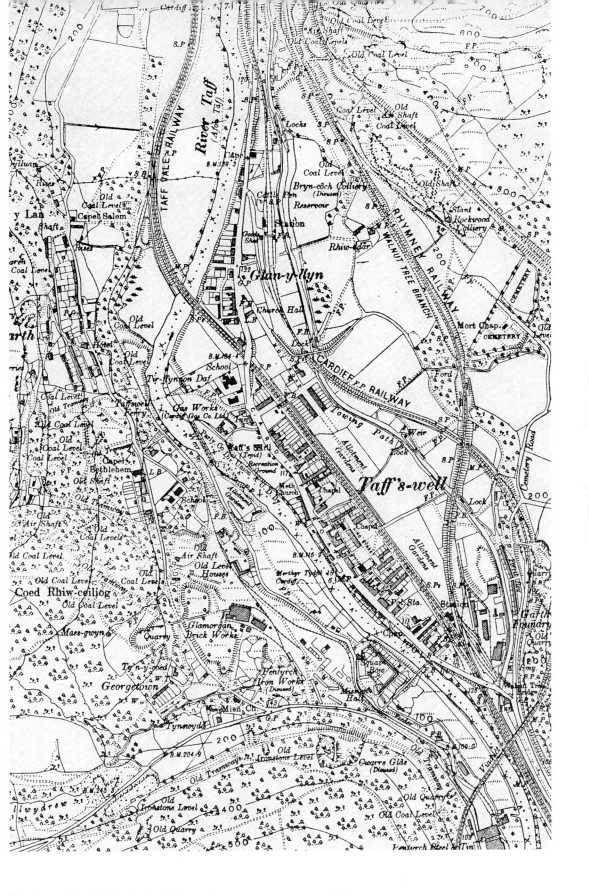

Top The wooden board surface of the down platform could be lethal to walk on when wet, so it is not surprising that it was later removed and replaced with tarmac. At the up platform engine No 5668 is waiting for the go-ahead with a passenger train on 26 July 1952; hand-signalling is in operation due to the disconnecting of signals while the construction of a new section of track to Nantgarw Coke Works is being laid; this would join up with the former Cardiff Railway line at Glan-y-llyn, thus allowing that company's line from Coryton to Glan-y-llyn to be closed. *The late S. Rickard, J and J collection*

Middle Looking down on the station from the footbridge on 25 August 1961, the station buildings ooze character. Sitting next to the waiting room door, some passengers are waiting for the train to Cardiff, although it looks as though the children are getting restless. The GWR gas lamps have been fitted with 'swan neck' adaptors for electric lighting. On the right the former Rhymney Railway's line up the 'big hill' towards Aber Junction can clearly be seen. *G. Pearce*

Bottom The second Walnut Tree Junction signal box was on the up side. It was opened in 1921 and closed over the weekend of 24/25 January 1997, and demolished by Railtrack in March 1997. On 13 April 1968 part of the booking office is just in view on the left. *J. Morgan*

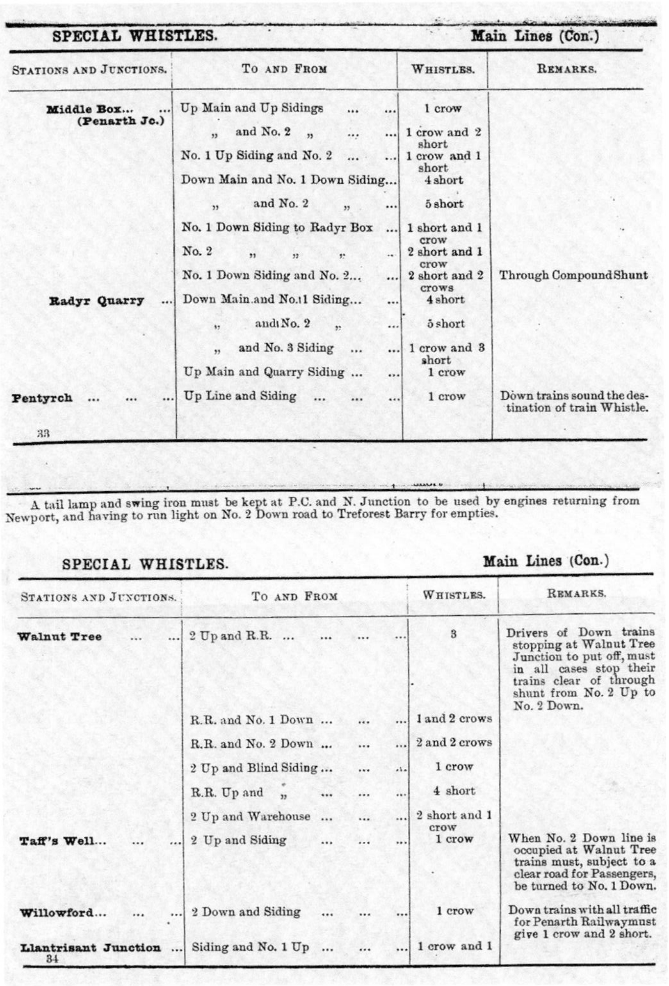

(Handwritten wagon order, reproduced sideways)

May 4th 1908

Thomas Edwards
Tynant Quarries
Taff's Well.

10 New 10 ton Wagons
with 2 side doors cut through to top
15ft long × 7ft wide × 2ft 6 deep all inside Measurements.
2" deal sheeting + battening. 4'6" × 1'8 planed, side door hatch
bolted through next nail only, Charley pattern (Brass Presses)
Lift Lever or Lock/tooth, 10" buffer. of Ironwork with long neck and
for slope in (Bearing Springs) Plates 4 × ⅞ Gauge Plank, seven
deep spring shaft (?)

on a 4 years lease at a rental of £ [10-2-0] coal wagon) for
Annual (payable quarterly.
Lease with the York Central Wagon Co. Ltd. Rotherham
at the price of £62-10-6 each out cost.

Painted dark colour. White Letters Shaded Black (on plate).

Thomas Edwards
Tynant Quarries
Taff's Well.

No. 13/22

Registered by T.V.R.
Bearing York Central Wagon Co. brown plates No's 60661/60670.

Delivered (to T.V.R. April 7 May 1908) (invoice 26 May 1908) (see sheet 161)

SPECIAL WHISTLES.		Main Lines (Con.)	
STATIONS AND JUNCTIONS.	TO AND FROM	WHISTLES.	REMARKS.
Middle Box. (Penarth Jc.)	Up Main and Up Sidings ...	1 crow	
	" and No. 2 " ...	1 crow and 2 short	
	No. 1 Up Siding and No. 2 ...	1 crow and 1 short	
	Down Main and No. 1 Down Siding...	4 short	
	" and No. 2 "	5 short	
	No. 1 Down Siding to Radyr Box	1 short and 1 crow	
	No. 2 "	2 short and 1 crow	
Radyr Quarry	No. 1 Down Siding and No. 2...	2 short and 2 crows	Through Compound Shunt
	Down Main and No.1 Siding...	4 short	
	" and No. 2 "	5 short	
	" and No. 3 Siding ...	1 crow and 3 short	
	Up Main and Quarry Siding ...	1 crow	
Pentyrch ...	Up Line and Siding ...	1 crow	Down trains sound the destination of train Whistle.

33

A tail lamp and swing iron must be kept at P.C. and N. Junction to be used by engines returning from Newport, and having to run light on No. 2 Down road to Treforest Barry for empties.

SPECIAL WHISTLES.		Main Lines (Con.)	
STATIONS AND JUNCTIONS.	TO AND FROM	WHISTLES.	REMARKS.
Walnut Tree ...	2 Up and R.R. ...	8	Drivers of Down trains stopping at Walnut Tree Junction to put off, must in all cases stop their trains clear of through shunt from No. 2 Up to No. 2 Down.
	R.R. and No. 1 Down ...	1 and 2 crows	
	R.R. and No. 2 Down ...	2 and 2 crows	
	2 Up and Blind Siding ...	1 crow	
	R.R. Up and "	4 short	
	2 Up and Warehouse ...	2 short and 1 crow	
Taff's Well ...	2 Up and Siding ...	1 crow	When No. 2 Down line is occupied at Walnut Tree trains must, subject to a clear road for Passengers, be turned to No. 1 Down. Down trains with all traffic for Penarth Railway must give 1 crow and 2 short.
Willowford ...	2 Down and Siding ...	1 crow	
Llantrisant Junction ...	Siding and No. 1 Up ...	1 crow and 1	

34

TVR code of engine whistles for the line through Taffs Well, 22 October 1894. *T. D. Chapman*

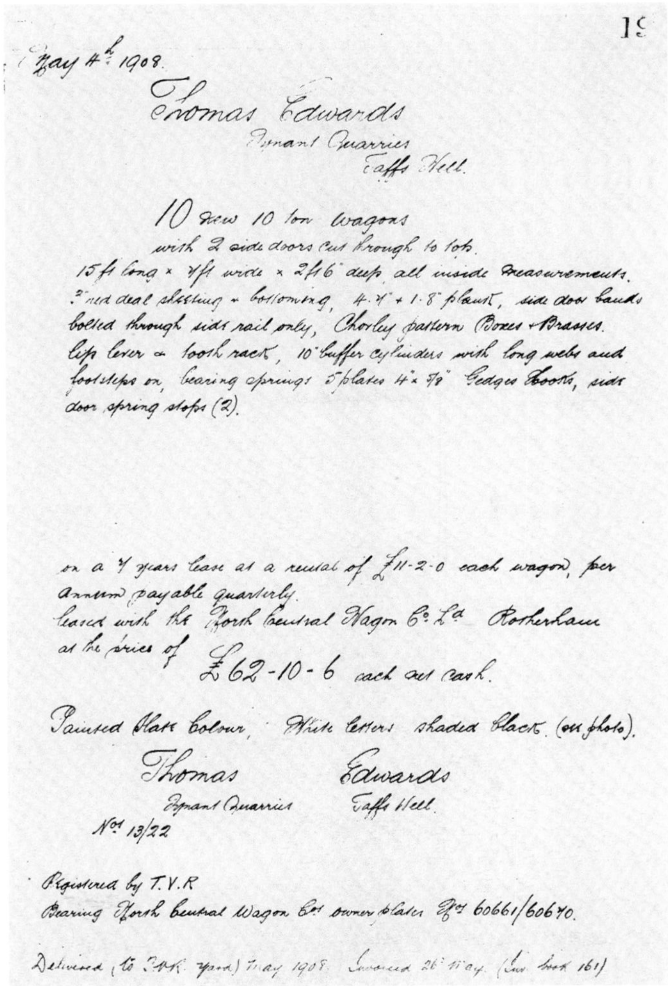

This wagon order, dated 4 May 1908, is for ten new wagons of 10-ton capacity, painted and worded for Messrs Thomas Edwards of Tynant Quarries, Taffs Well. *Powell Duffryn Wagon Company*

FALL FROM TAFF TRAIN.

An action alleging negligence and claiming damages against the Taff Vale Railway Company came on for hearing on Wednesday at Cardiff Assizes (before Mr. Justice Eldon Bankes and a jury), the plaintiff being Mrs. Elizabeth Morgan, wife of William Morgan, a collier, 5, Neville Houses, Pentyrch, who sought to recover damages for personal injuries sustained through the company's alleged negligence whilst travelling on their railway on the night of Saturday, February 11th, 1911.

The defendant company denied negligence, and set up the defence that plaintiff herself was guilty of contributory negligence. Mr. Abel Thomas, K.C., M.P., and Mr. A. T. James (instructed by Mr. Stanley Jones, Pontypridd) appeared for the plaintiff; Mr. Benjamin Francis-Williams, K.C., and Mr. H. O. C. Beasley (instructed by Messrs. Ingledew) defended.

Mr. Abel Thomas, in opening, said plaintiff was 36 years of age, and had four children. Up to the time of the accident she was strong, healthy and active, and also was a very clever woman with her needle, making 10s. a week by her work as a dressmaker. She often had to come to Cardiff for the things she required, and on the evening in question, at about seven o'clock, she took train for Taff Well. Just before the train started a man came up to the door of the third class compartment Mrs. Morgan had entered, and, seeing a woman there alone, he did not enter, and plaintiff was not sure whether he turned the handle or not. At the next station (Radyr) no one came to the door, and the train started. Almost immediately plaintiff was in the act of pulling up the window, and as the train was leaving the platform the door swung open. Plaintiff grasped at the door and shouted. Her hand slipped, and she dropped on some stones by the side of the railway, and was for a time unconscious. She was assisted on to the platform by the only porter at the station and by some stranger who saw what had happened. She was taken to the office of the stationmaster, who asked her a good many questions, and the reports he made they had never seen. When plaintiff got better she said she would like to see a doctor, and the porter took her across the line to the surgery of Dr. R. Thomas, and in his absence the assistant examined her, and did not think there was much the matter except that she was very much shaken, and she went on to Cardiff. Soon she felt herself getting worse, and returned home in great pain, and almost up till now she had been in the same state. Mrs. Morgan was an out-patient at the infirmary until September last, and was now little more than a physical wreck.

Plaintiff's appearance in the witness-box and her description of her symptoms indicated that she had suffered no little discomfort. She wore spectacles, and explained that she could not bear artificial light; her hearing also was defective, and so was her memory, so that now she could not do her sewing as before, and she had to get assistance to do the housework.

Dr. Daniel Rees Thomas, Taffs Well, who had known plaintiff for twelve years, agreed that prior to the accident she was a strong, healthy woman, but now her hearing, eyesight, and memory were affected, and her left arm had lost much of its power. In his opinion her present condition was due to the accident.

Dr. Hamilton, formerly house surgeon at Cardiff Infirmary, and now of Manchester, also gave evidence as to the plaintiff's condition, which he attributed to injuries received in an accident such as had been described.

For the defence Mr. Francis-Williams submitted that the accident could not have happened as described, and that, as the door was fastened, there had been no negligence on the part of the railway company.

David Beavan, stationmaster at Radyr, said plaintiff came to him of her own accord and lodged a complaint.

Mr. Abel Thomas read the report of the occurrence submitted by the witness to headquarters, in which he said Mrs. Morgan explained to him that "she went to the door to look out and in doing so she leant against the door with the result that it opened, and she fell out."

Mr. Abel Thomas: Didn't she say she was lifting up the window?—No, sir.

Are you sure of it?—I am positive.

What did you say when she said it? Did you say it was impossible?—No, I did not.

What did you say when she said she leant against the door and it fell open?—I did not express any opinion.

Mr. Abel Thomas: You expressed the opinion on the Monday that she had no claim?

His Lordship: We have not got so far as that.

Mr. Abel Thomas (to witness): You expressed the opinion that she had no claim?—I don't think so.

Annie Jones, Radyr, said she was standing on the platform when the train left and saw a woman in the rear end of the train looking out of the window and waving her arms. She did not know who the woman was.

Cross-examined: Witness admitted her father was an engine driver on the Taff Vale Railway. The woman she saw was waving her arms, although there was no one on the platform at the time but witness and a porter.

Tudor Morgan, porter, at Radyr, also gave evidence as to finding plaintiff after the accident.

William Hando, the guard, was called to prove that all the doors were fastened before the train left Radyr. He did not see anyone hanging out of one of the doors and did not hear of the accident until very much later in the evening. Plaintiff was standing at the window when the train reached Radyr and when it left.

Dr. Edward Joscelyne, medical officer to the Taff Vale Railway Company, said he examined plaintiff on July 10th. All her symptoms were subjective. He did not think her deafness was caused by the accident. The diminution in the grip of the left hand compared with the right was merely subjective. He did not think Mrs. Morgan suffered from nervousness.

The jury, after retiring, found for plaintiff for £125.

This page An unfortunate mishap reported in the *Pontypridd Observer*, 30 March 1912. *Pontypridd Library*

Right A ganger dies on the line: from the Pontypridd Observer, 5 November 1921. *Pontypridd Library*

Opposite top Mr John Price, wearing his trilby hat, is carefully supervising a permanent way gang at Taffs Well Sidings circa 1920; as a tea boy he had worked with his father on the same stretch of this line nearly 40 years earlier. These sidings were located just north of the village of Taffs Well. *Courtesy of Miss C. M. Price and Mr J. Roberts*

Opposite middle Caught in full flight on a glass plate negative, midway between the second and first Taffs Well stations, is TVR engine No 91 hauling a train of four former railmotor coaches forming a Cardiff to Pontypridd service in 1922. No 91 was built at the Vulcan Foundry in 1921, works number 3495, and was renumbered as 351 by the GWR; it was rebuilt with a taper boiler in 1929, and withdrawn from service in 1956. In the far distance can be seen the Barry Railway viaduct. The down relief line from Pontypridd to Taffs Well was taken out of use in 1968, and the up relief line from Taffs Well to Maesmawr was clipped out of use in August 1978, but not lifted until December 1980. *LCGB, Ken Nunn Collection*

FATAL ACCIDENT.

Alleged Lack of Appliances.

A distressing fatal accident occurred on the Taff Vale railway about half a mile below the Treforest station on Friday morning of last week, when Harry Atwell, of Taff's Well, was killed by a passenger train.

It appears that he was the signalman of the gang which was working on the line, and that in stepping out of the way of two coal trains he stepped in front of the 10.20 passenger train from Cardiff and was instantly killed. He was dragged for some distance before the train could pull up. He received severe injuries to the body and his head was battered to pieces.

We learn from a reliable source that when the deceased was taken to the Treforest Station on a board with his flag over his head, a volunteer came forward to bandage the body, but (it is stated)) there was not an inch of bandage either at the junction or the station. No stretcher was at the station to take the deceased home, and he was lying upon the board on the station from the time the accident occurred until 11.22, when appliances came down from Pontypridd. If these allegations are correct they are to be regretted, for although in this case thea ccident proved fatal, there is always a possibility this case the accident proved ing, and the necessity for surgical appliances at such a busy station at Treforest is obvious.

Right This was the original station house at Taffs Well and the site of its first station, opened in October 1840 and closed on 22 June 1863 with the opening of the second station. Seen here on 6 September 1967, today it has been modernised almost beyond recognition. The photograph was taken from the skew road bridge that crossed the line carrying the Cardiff Road through Taffs Well; this bridge, No 33, was built with local Blue Pennant rough dressed stone, and carried an E. Finch & Co bridge plaque, dated 1905. In June 1992 this former TVR bridge was made redundant and replaced with a modern steel structure. *D. G. Thomas*

Left Taffs Well Sidings signal box, where the private Melin Griffith line made its northern connection with TVR metals. The Melin Griffith tin works and the Eagle Foundry, also on this private line, supplied the TVR with many useful parts, including cast-iron parts for footbridges. This signal box was built in 1884, and closed on 4 October 1964. The rough track at the rear of the box climbs up the hill to Ynyscoi Farm, while a short distance northwards is the site of the former Ynyscoi Tunnel, named after it. The tunnel was opened in 1840, and was wide enough for a single line to pass through, but between 1857 and 1859 it was excavated out to become a cutting, allowing plans to lay a double track to proceed; in 1860 the cutting was again widened to enable the double track to be quadrupled. *A. G. Powell*

Below A bird's-eye view of an 82XX Class engine and train near Taffs Well Sidings signal box on 16 June 1955. *The late S. Rickard, J and J collection*

Treforest

Above Treforest Industrial Estate station was opened by the GWR in 1942 on an island platform, reached by two passageways, one the entrance, the other the exit; both went under the down line to reach the road below. This is the view looking north towards Upper Boat Power Station, providing a good view of the up main line, with the up and down relief lines to the left. At road level on the right is a house, next to which are steps that take pedestrians to the nearby Treforest Industrial Estate. The station was later reduced to halt status and, as seen in this 1960 photograph, the name was changed to Treforest Estate. *Lens of Sutton Collection*

Below This iron girder bridge carried the rails of the Treforest Industrial Estate over the River Taff to the Leiner bone-crushing works and Rosedale Sidings. This essential bridge was used not only for railway traffic but also quite regularly by pedestrians to reach the factories they worked in. The bridge was located a few steps down the slope from the Industrial Estate station, and is still in place today; even the wooden planks that cover the deck show no signs of wear. This was not part of the TVR main line as such, but was used by the GWR traffic to deliver to and pick up from the factories. Built by Dorman Long, this bridge was so important during the Second World War that this photograph was included in the navigators' instructional pouch, numbered GB7, as one of the Luftwaffe targets for its bombers on 30 November 1941. *Pontypridd Library*

Above Maesmawr station was opened in April 1845 but closed in July as a failed experiment that did not live up to expectations. Located next to the road known as Tonteg Hill, there is no trace of it today, and it is only with local knowledge that the site of this short-lived station can be found. From just south of Maesmawr signal box, opened by the GWR in 1930, sidings led to Upper Boat Power Station, part of which is seen here on 25 October 1956 being passed by the 11.00am Merthyr to Barry Island service, headed by No 5643 carrying its 'JD' target. This engine was permanently shedded at Abercynon; built at Swindon in 1925, it was withdrawn in July 1963, eventually passing into preservation in September 1971.

On 6 December 1972 Class 37 No D6929 made a trial run over the power station sidings and down to the power station itself in the hope of transferring surplus stock to Llynfi Power Station by rail, but unfortunately this scheme did not materialise. On 21 May 1974 three of the four chimneys were demolished, and the fourth on the 31st. The cooling tower came down on 10 June 1974, and in November-December the power station siding tracks were cut up into 3-foot lengths and the metal sent to Germany for smelting down. The power station was finally demolished in 1976, and Top Sidings, at Maesmawr, leading down to Treforest

Estate Sidings, were taken out of use in the same year. *The late S. Rickard, J and J collection*

Below This painting of Treforest Tin Works circa 1850 by Mr J. Appleby was presented to Mr William Crawshay, of Cyfathfa Castle, Merthyr Tydfil, by the publisher and printer Mr J. J. Purchase. On the left can be glimpsed the silhouette of a Taff Vale Railway engine, pulling what seems to be quite a long train – perhaps a little artistic licence has been used. The tin works were opened and producing in 1834, and a siding was put in to serve them at an unknown date. The last owner of the site to use rail traffic was Messrs P. Leiner & Sons, who also had a rail connection on the Treforest Estate. By that time the former tin works buildings were being used for the crushing of bones, which came from India and were loaded into railway wagons at Cardiff Docks then transported to the factory. This rail service ceased in 1963, when Leiners decided to use road transport. At present the works are being protected from vandalism as there are plans to restore them to preservation status as a Grade 1 listed building. *Pontypridd Library*

Opposite An Ordnance Survey map of 1943, showing Treforest station. There were once two junctions here. On the down side, south of the station, was a short-lived connection with the Cardiff Railway; after the ceremonial opening train of 1909, the junction was taken up by the TVR because of a dispute with the Cardiff Railway, which then had to terminate its line on the east side of its impressive viaduct at Rhydyfelin. On the up side, coming down from Tonteg Junction, was the Barry Railway line, which opened in 1889 and can be seen at the bottom of the map. Today a 'park and ride' facility covers the relief lines and coal yard, and on the former marshalling yard there is a car park for the Polytechnic of Wales. *Crown copyright*

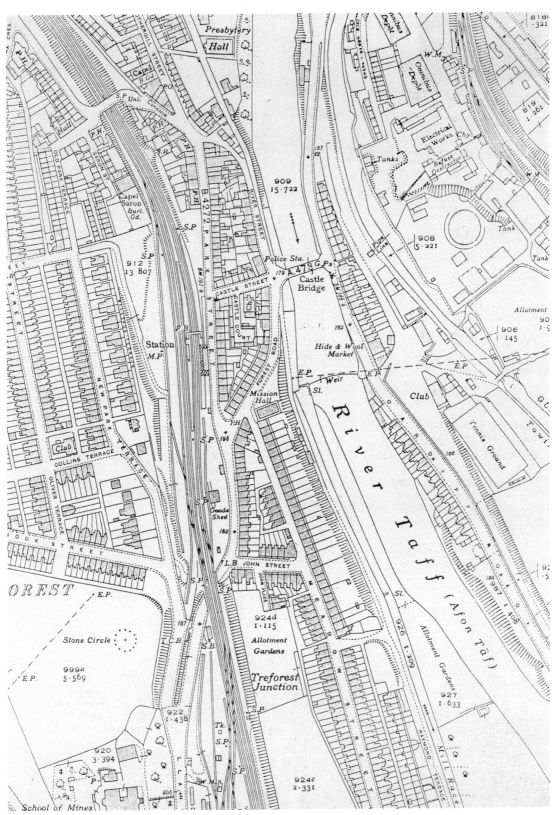

Top Treforest station and goods shed were opened in 1845. *Slaters Directory* of 1880 states that Mr F. Hawkins was Station Master, while in 1893 a TVR passenger train went over the embankment at Treforest and 12 people lost their lives. On 18 March 1908 the down buildings were destroyed by fire, including the booking office, causing the death of a woman. The station is still in use for passenger services. This is the view looking south circa 1969; by now the original TVR up waiting room has been replaced. Note that there is not one sweet paper or empty crisp packet to be seen on the platforms or track, a far cry from the state of some stations today! In the distance is Treforest Junction signal box. *Lens of Sutton Collection*

Above left The down-side buildings were very grand, especially when compared to the up-side waiting room, seen here on the left on 12 October 1963. *L. D. Bryant*

Above From the *Pontypridd Observer*, 27 February 1904. *Pontypridd Library*

Left On 15 October 1973 British Rail announced, under the heading of further station improvement, that at Treforest the station buildings on the down platform (used by trains travelling towards Cardiff), would be replaced by a brick-built waiting shelter and ticket office, and lighting would be improved. This view, facing north towards Pontypridd, dates from 1969. Today the area behind the platform is a park and ride area. *Lens of Sutton Collection*

Former GWR No 4117 waits for the signal to depart from Treforest with a passenger train for Treherbert some time in 1949. This 5101 Class engine was built in 1936 and withdrawn from service in 1961. *S. Fisher*

Pontypridd

Pontypridd station was originally known as Newbridge, and was located just south of the High Street in Pontypridd town. Comprising a single platform, it opened on 8 October 1840 to freight traffic, and the following day for passenger services; this station later became the site of the cattle pens. Access to the platform was via Station Street, and this area is now part of the Pontypridd Magistrates Court grounds. Plans for a new station were announced in the *Cardiff Times* on 11 November 1856, and that year Newbridge station was renamed Pontypridd. By 1862 the up platform had been extended north of the High Street, and on 15 July 1863 all trains were directed to use this platform, thus avoiding the need to cross the lines. On 13 October 1865 the *Cardiff Times* reported that a new platform was being constructed on the down side, and the erecting of a footbridge had started. This new platform was north of High Street, with the old platform south of High Street being retained and extended; thus the new layout

was an island platform and one facing platform on the town side.

Further reconstruction took place in 1891. Mr Ammon Beasley was appointed TVR General Manager on 30 September of that year, and under his supervision the station layout was converted into three through platform faces. In the TVR timetable booklet for July, August and September 1892, the station is referred to as Pontypridd Junction, and the Station Master Mr William Felton. His death was reported in 1899, the same year when a collision took place at Pontypridd station, injuring 15 people.

Further major rebuilding and reconstruction began in 1907; this was to be a completely new

Pontypridd Observer, 27 May 1899. *Pontypridd Library*

Pontypridd Chronicle, 12 January 1884. *Pontypridd Library*

T.V.R. STATION.—It appears that the inhabitants have at last prevailed upon the Taff Vale Railway Company to enlarge and improve their station here. This will be acceptable to all, for the the present station is a poor apology for the convenience and comfort of the passengers. Perhaps it would be as well also just to remind the stationmaster that it would be advisable, under the present circumstances, to take off the terrible paper with "Private" written upon it from the waiting-room doors, and to keep the doors unlocked for the convenience of those who have a right to them.

MR. FELTON SHOT.

On Thursday evening Sergeant Rees was called to Mr Felton's office at the Taff Vale Railway station. On proceeding to the spot he founh Mr Felton and Dr Roach. Mr Felton was groaning and said he wanted to die. He told them not to tell his wife that he had shot himself. Dr Howard Davies soon after arrived and attended to him. He found that he had been shot on the left side just below the heart. The bullet had entered the body, passed out at the back, and became embedded in the desk. Mr Felton was taken by special train to Cardiff infirmary. In the room was found a six chambered revolver, four chambers of which had been discharged. Miss Bowen (Refreshment Rooms) heard a shot fired and she informed David Bevan, who rushed to the office, and a doctor was sent for. Mr Felton died at 1 p.m. on Friday from the effects of the wound.

layout, much larger and longer than before, with the new Alexandra Docks Railway bay and the new down platform completed by March 1910. The new station was opened by HM King George V and Queen Mary in June 1912; although the station was not yet finished, this was a grand occasion with all the TVR Directors in attendance. It was not until 28 July 1914 that the reconstruction was completed, and in total the station now had seven platform faces: two through lines and five bays. The GWR named it Pontypridd Central to distinguish it from the Barry Railway station at Pontypridd Graig.

On 13 January 1969 British Rail announced that several South Wales stations would be grant-aided, with the provision of facilities for the weather protection of passengers. The size and antiquated condition of many of the buildings, aggravated by vandalism, made maintenance very costly and necessitated a policy of demolishing many of the waiting rooms and the removal of other facilities from some of the lesser-used stations. It was, however, decided that some form of shelter for passengers be retained or provided at the following Taff Vale stations: Abercynon, Cardiff Bute Road, Dinas Rhondda, Dingle Road Halt, Llandaff, Llwynypia, Merthyr, Merthyr Vale, Penarth, Pentrebach, Pontypridd, Porth, Quakers Yard, Radyr, Taffs Well, Tonypandy & Trealaw,

Treforest, Treforest Estate, Trehafod, Treherbert, Treorchy, Troedyrhiw, and Ystrad Rhondda. The cost of this scheme was given as £120,000 in 1969, but it had reached £150,000 by 1970, and £240,000 by 1973; two years later the cost of this station reconstruction programme had increased to three-quarters of a million pounds, but it would improve conditions at most of the 46 stations involved over the ensuing four years to 1979.

On 3 April 1974 it was reported that the Secretary of State for Wales, Mr John Morris QC MP, had decided to make a grant of £56,000 to British Rail towards the cost of modernising Pontypridd station. The improvements, costing a total of £113,000, would include a modern station entrance at street level, improvements to the subway steps and walls leading to the platform, conversion of part of the existing toilets for use by the disabled, and modernisation of the forecourt and station facade.

On 22 February 1990 plans were approved by Mid Glamorgan Council for further development. In recent years only one section of the very long platform had been in use, and new work would include a footbridge, waiting shelter and ramped pedestrian access from High Street, while the platform would be surfaced with red and charcoal grey pavior blocks. Work started in July 1990, and was ready for public use in September 1991.

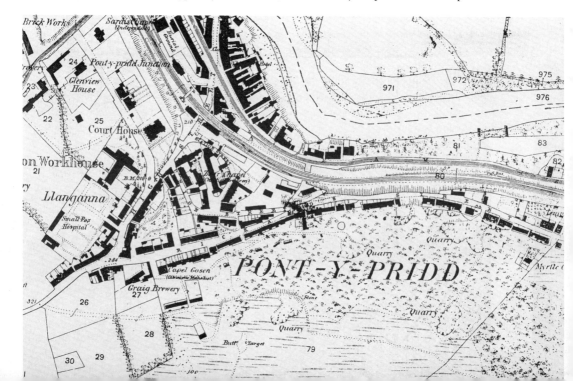

Below left 'Pont-y-Pridd Junction' on an Ordnance Survey map of 1874. *Crown copyright*

Above This 1893 photograph shows Pontypridd station in the foreground and the River Taff in the background. Nearest the camera are wagons of the Aberdare Coal Company, which seem to be mixture of 10-ton and some 6-ton vehicles of the 'dumb buffer' variety, all carrying timber planks and pit props, probably of Scandinavian origin, hauled here from Cardiff Docks. A temporary timber platform is being erected, possibly the start of work on excavation of the hillside at the west side of the station to allow the relief lines to be laid; this would eventually relieve traffic congestion, which was what the rebuilding programme, started in 1891, was all about. Work on the relief sidings began at the southern end of the station in 1893, the first relief line was finished in 1900, and the second in October 1901. Behind the Aberdare wagons is what is believed to be TVR engine

No 9, built in 1879, formerly sold by the LB&SCR in 1882 to the ANDR, acquired by the TVR from the latter in the early 1890s, and reported to have carried the name *Pontypridd*. Next to the engine is a former brake-van of Rhymney Railway origin. *Pontypridd Library*

Below A hillside view of the station circa 1904, shortly before reconstruction as one long island platform, showing in the distance the lines to the Rhondda going to the left, and the main line to Merthyr gently curving at the right across Brunel's viaduct. In the middle foreground can be seen the temporary wooden platform with a number of buildings, one of which will house the kitchen facilities for use by the construction workers (the platform seems to be in the same position as the one seen in the previous photograph). The new relief lines can be clearly seen on the left, western, side of the station. *C. W. Harris*

Opposite above This view is looking south, circa 1910, during the reconstruction begun in 1907, and shows the down main lines. The new roof girders are in position on the right on the island platform of 1862. In the background, through the latticework of the girders, can be seen the up and down relief lines, and on the left is the former down platform of 1862, with its original roof still in position. The temporary platform at the far end of the island carries the huts used by the contractors, and in front of them a distinguished group of TVR officials are watching the progress, probably the main reason for a photographer being on site. Among them, but too far away to identify exactly where they stand, is Mr Ammon Beasley, TVR General Manager, the Marquess of Bute, and Mr A. E. Giles, TVR Chairman. Despite the presence of the officials, the contractors are not letting the opportunity to be captured on camera pass by! *J. Dore-Dennis collection*

Opposite below Facing in the opposite direction, this photo gives a good view of the shuttering and infill needed to raise the platform edges to their new height. Once again the TVR officials are in the picture, while over on the right are some loco coal wagons, and a steam crane beyond. The reconstruction work rose the level of the station by nearly 5 feet, an amazing piece of engineering, carried out, as can be seen, with steam cranes and a lot of manual labour. *J. Dore-Dennis collection*

Above left In this overall view of the finished station, circa 1914, on the left can be seen once again the relief lines, while bottom left are the cattle pens, occupying the former site of the 1840s station. Next to the pens was a subway through which cattle and livestock were driven down to the slaughterhouse on the Broadway, opposite the subway entrance. *Author's collection*

Above right From the *Pontypridd Observer*, 7 August 1915. *Pontypridd Library*

Below This photograph, taken from the low wall in Rickard Street in 1956, has captured a 'B Set' – two permanently coupled Brake 3rds – in the carriage sidings beyond the station roof. Nearer the camera a rake of full coal wagons slowly passes the cattle pens on its way up valley. On the left can be seen part of the massive retaining wall that skirts the outward edge of the relief sidings. It looks like a 'good drying day' – pity about the smoke drifting towards the washing on the line! *The late S. Rickard, J and J collection*

The Royal Train stands at Pontypridd station in 1976, drawn by a pair of Class 31 diesels on the return journey from the official opening of an extension to the Hoover factory at Merthyr Tydfil, which was performed by HRH Prince Charles. The train is about to depart after its short stop en route to Cardiff. *M. Davies*

Mr John Price, Permanent Way Inspector, stands proudly outside his office at Pontypridd circa 1923. This was the former booking office, and alongside can be seen the Signal & Telegraph office. On the right are empty coal wagons on the up relief road, being returning to one of the valley collieries. *Courtesy of Miss C. M. Price and Mr J. Roberts*

In bay platform number 7, the Newport and Cowbridge bay, Fireman Arthur Leaworthy leans from the cab of 2-4-0T No 3586. This engine was the last survivor of the GWR 3500 'Metro' Class, built in 1899 to works number 1738, and was used regularly on the service to Cowbridge. Photographed in 1946, No 3586 was withdrawn from service in 1949. Mr Leaworthy was stationed at Llantrisant depot from 1930 to 1948, and worked on auto-trains between Llantrisant and Pontypridd, and Abercynon and Tonypandy. *A. Leaworthy*

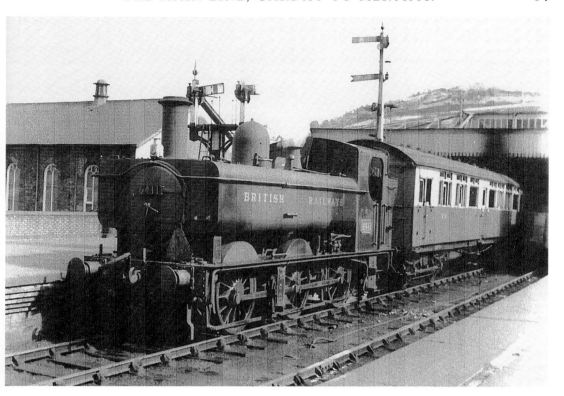

Above At the north end of Pontypridd station on 11 September 1951, Pannier tank No 6411 heads trailer No 114 en route for the Ynysybwl line; this combination was regularly seen on that branch for many years. This former GWR 6400 Class engine was built at Swindon in 1934 and withdrawn in 1961. *R. M. Casserley*

Right Pontypridd was possibly the most important station on the Taff Vale Railway network, and hopefully a little of the atmosphere of this busy station has been captured in these pictures. Also on 11 September 1951 engine No 344, bearing its 'CO' target, takes on water. The great height of the retaining wall was clearly an impressive feat of engineering construction. The plaque on the bridge spanning High Street shows that it is another by E. Finch Co, and is dated 1899. A local saying about this station was that it was the highest in the world – above the Half Moon, but below the Rising Sun, both of which were of course public houses, located east and west of the station in High Street. No 344 was formerly TVR No 12 of the 'A' Class, built by Hawthorn Leslie in 1914, works number 3061, reboilered by the GWR with a taper boiler in 1930, and withdrawn from service in 1952. *R. M. Casserley*

Right TVR luggage label. *L. D. Bryant*

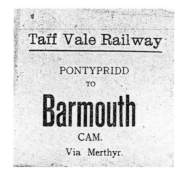

Taff Vale Railway

PONTYPRIDD

TO

Barmouth

CAM.

Via Merthyr.

Below Graham Cumpston (left) a former Radyr-based driver, now retired, shakes the hand of Senior Railman Relief Alun Powell, now retired but seen here in charge of Pontypridd station in September 1991, while Val Powell has her head turned away. After serving as signalman, then freight guard, Alun never looked smarter! Behind them ar the steps leading down to street level. The Red Star parcel office on the right, like all the platform buildings, is in re terracotta and brick, while the support for the massive roof also act a rainwater drains, an idea copied from Brunel's design at Paddington. Thi photo gives a clear indication of wha was in the minds of the architects back in 1907 – while working in wet mudd conditions and in ever-present dange of being struck by a passing train, the could picture what we see today.

As Senior Railman Relief, Alun covered station and booking office duties not only at Pontypridd and Merthyr, but also at Porth, Tonypandy Treforest, Taffs Well, Radyr, Llandaf and Cathays, and signal lamp dutie from Llandaff to Porth, Pontypridd to Black Lion, Ystrad Mynach and Bargoed, as well as Red Star parcel duties at Pontypridd and Merthyr. He and two others – Mel Davies and Chris Scaplehorn – covered these duties during holiday and sick periods, and they were issued with passes to travel on all the valley lines from Pontypridd which meant working a 12-hour day; it also very often meant working on a Sunday at Pontypridd or Merthyr Alun's favourite job was working in the booking office at Aberdare. *Author*

Left The street-level entrance and forecourt of Pontypridd station on 13 April 1968. The large British Rail van seen at the end of the forecourt is a BMC Morris FG. *D. G. Thomas*

Below left On the forecourt in February 1961, British Railways van

driver Mr Eric Coleman stands next to his Thorneycroft delivery vehicle No 3599W. As can be seen on the side of the van, the cinema is showing that great classic *Ben-Hur* – who can forget the camera-work in that brilliant chariot race! *E. C. Coleman*

Opposite bottom right Pontypridd parcels driver for the Graig area and Pontypridd town, Mr Phil Hopkins, is seen either up the Graig, or in Hopkinstown, with his Morris Commercial in 1964. Being a van driver always gave you the chance to go home for dinner – well, most times. *R. Burgess and R. Rose*

Above Gas lights are in abundance in this scene at Pontypridd Junction at the north end of the station in June 1921. In the centre of the junction is the large 230-lever signal box, and next to it the water tower; the photograph was taken from bay platforms 3 and 4. On the hillside is Graigwen, the 'white hill', and behind the water tower can be seen the Millfield Hotel. This junction was the TVR's southern entrance to the Rhondda, on the left, while on the right the main line crossed the viaduct and went north to Merthyr. In the foreground are the hose-pipes attached to a gas supply, piped from a gas tank, used for the filling of gas cylinders located under coaches that were using the bay; the hoses were in use right up to the late 1950s. *The late S. Rickard, J and J collection*

Below Looking from the junction in towards the station on 8 August 1965, the spur leading to the Maritime Colliery can be seen on the right. The Maritime Colliery was opened in 1844 as the Newbridge Colliery, under the ownership of a Mr Calvert. *D. G. Thomas*

SPECIAL WHISTLES.

Main Lines (Con.)

STATIONS AND JUNCTIONS.	TO AND FROM	WHISTLES.	REMARKS.
Llantrisant Junction ...	Siding and No. 2 Up	1 crow and 2	
	Tin Works and No. 1 Down	1 crow	
	South Sidings and Branch	1 crow	
Treforest Barry	Forest Steel and No. 2 Up	1 crow and 2 short	See Special Instructions, pages 22 and 23.
	Warehouse and No. 1 Down	1 crow and 1 short	
	Barry Up and Down and vice versa ...	4 short	
	Barry Up Line Sidings... ...	1 crow	
Treforest North	Forest Steel Works Siding	4 short	
P. C. & N. Railway			See Appendix.
P. C. & N. Junction ...	Main Lines	3 and 1 crow	
	Bay Road and Branch	1 crow and 1 short	Down Main Line Trains will use the Standard Whistle for the road upon which they require to travel
35	„ and Down Line	1 crow and 2 short	

A tail lamp and swing iron must be kept at P.C. and N. Junction to be used by engines returning from Newport, and having to run light on No. 2 Down road to Treforest Barry for empties.

SPECIAL WHISTLES.

Main Lines (Con.)

STATIONS AND JUNCTIONS.	TO AND FROM	WHISTLES.	REMARKS.
P. C. & N. Junction ...	Old Warehouse Siding...	4 short	
Pontypridd Junction ...	Rhondda Branch	3	
	Chapel Siding	1 crow	
	Down Branch and Bay...	2	
	Up „ „	2 and 1 short	
	Penrhiew Siding	1 crow and 1 short	
	Down Main and Down Branch ...	4 short	
	Crawshay's Sidings and Bay	1 crow and 2 short	

SPECIAL WHISTLES.

Rhondda Branches.

	TO AND FROM	WHISTLES.	REMARKS.
	All Colliery Sidings not otherwise provided for by Special Whistle	1 crow.	
Rhondda Cutting ...	To Down Main Line	3	
36	To Down Rhondda Bay	2	

Left   TVR code of engine whistle through Pontypridd, 22 October 1894
T. D. Chapman

Below   An Ordnance Survey map of 1874 providing an overall view of the Pontypridd Junction layout. *Crown copyright*

Right   The same area seen in 1900 – note the development of the goods yard top right. *Crown copyright*

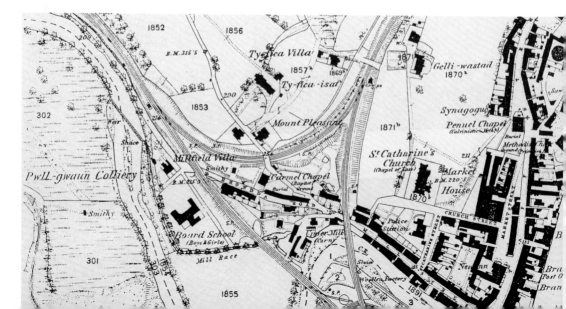

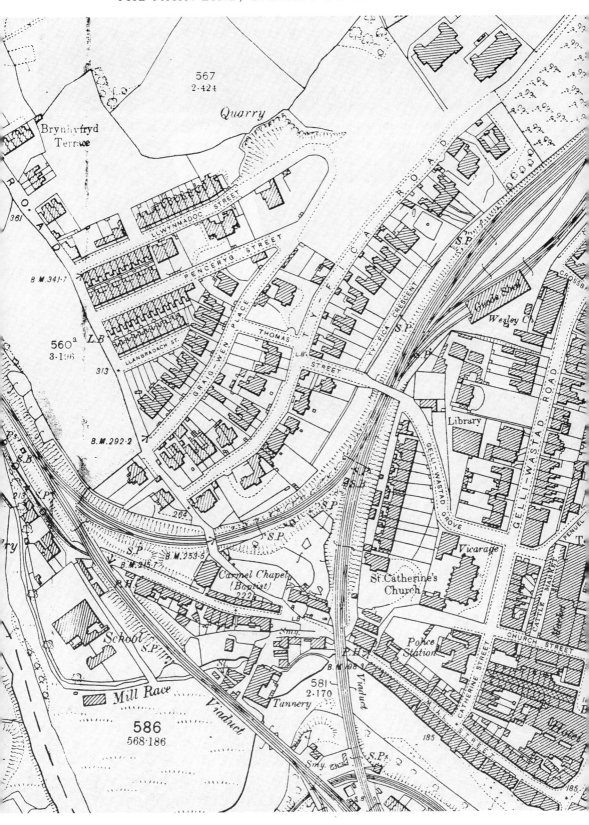

Left Passing the Rhondda cutting a Northern Junction is a mixed train en route to Abercynon and beyond circa 1923; there are GWR clerestor coaches at the front and TVR stock a the rear, and the van behind the engine is a TVR Full Brake. Pontypridd Northern Junction signal box can jus be seen above the second vehicle, while the line in left foreground is the connection to the goods yard. *Miss C M. Price and Mr J. Roberts*

Right Pontypridd goods yard was opened in 1889, and while the station was only a short distance away, this location was not frequently visited by enthusiasts, yet the viewpoint from the bridge at Thomas Street (seen here in the distance) or along the embankment at Tyfica Crescent was second to none. This view shows 5700 Class No 4662 carrying out shunting duties in the goods yard circa 1963; this engine was built in 1943 and withdrawn in 1965. *J. Morgan*

Below Another 5700 Class Pannier tank is shunting at Pontypridd goods yard. No 9622 was built in 1945 and withdrawn in 1965. *J. Morgan*

bove This close-up shows 1600 Class No 1655 hard at work under the fireman's watchful eyes. This engine was built by BR in 1955, and withdrawn from service a mere ten years later. *J. Morgan*

elow left From the *Pontypridd Observer*, 21 May 1921. *ontypridd Library*

elow right This view of the yard and its sidings dates from *irca* 1954. The yard had a Pooley weighbridge, inscribed *s* number 524 and dated 1925, to weigh a 20-ton *aximum* load – the weighbridge cabin can be seen behind *ne* crane. It is hard to believe that all of this is now gone, with only the main line running past. Demolition began in September 1984 and by January 1985 the sidings had been lifted and the ground cleared of the wooden sleepers. The area was then turned into a car park, run by Taff Ely Council, while the goods shed itself was gutted – even the unique TVR inscriptions on the roof supports were scrapped, leaving a skeleton structure that was rebuilt into an indoor bowls club. It would have been a great opportunity to have linked it with the Lewis Merthyr Colliery, part of the Welsh Heritage Centre, via Pontypridd Northern Junction and the nearby Rhondda cutting, to make this area into a working steam centre. *Ordnance Survey Department, Pontypridd*

Above Pontypridd goods depot staff in 1923, still in mixed TVR and GWR uniforms. Left to right, as recalled by C. Browne) they are:

Back row: I. Phillips, J. Davey, H. Murley, F. Ferris, F. Stearn, E. Ried, C. Browne; second row: F. Roberts, J. Eveis, G. Coates, D. Donovan, H. Trembath, H. Mansfield and one unknown; front row: W. Williams, A. Morris, W. Rees, Captain A. Williams (Goods Agent), A. Cresswell, P. Brennan (Foreman), J. O. Farreh, H. Richards.

The records show that in 1892 the Pontypridd Good Agent was Mr J. Roberts, and from at least 1903 to 1923 M A. Williams was the Goods Agent in charge. *P. Davies*

Below Class 37 No 37308 passes the site of Pontyprid goods yard on 16 April 1987. In the background is Tyfic Crescent, a good photographic viewpoint. The train is th 1.27pm MGR hoppers, probably en route to Abercwmbo Phurnacite Plant. *Author*

Abercynon

The remainder of the main line from Pontypridd to Merthyr Tydfil opened in stages: the line to Abercynon opened in October 1840, and by 12 April 1841 it had reached the TVR's Plymouth Street station at Merthyr. This section was ultimately doubled throughout by 1862, with a second viaduct, built alongside the 1840 one, at Quakers Yard.

Top Another Class 37, No 37251, heads south towards Pontypridd in August 1985 after coming off the Ynysybwl branch with fully loaded coal wagons from the Lady Windsor Colliery. On the right is the trackbed of the former Pont Shon Norton branch. *Author*

Middle and bottom This is Stormstown Junction, the northern point of Clydach Court Junction, a triangular-shaped junction with the Ynysybwl branch. The signal box is seen from a carriage window of a passing train en route to Pontypridd, on 3 June 1968.

The signal box closed on Sunday 4 September 1977, and on the left of this August 1985 photograph, looking south, is the trackbed of the line from Ynysdwr Junction, which joined the main line southbound having crossed Stormstown Viaduct (see page 119); as can be seen, this has been recently lifted. An MGR coal train from the Lady Windsor Colliery is approaching on the northbound chord from Ynysybwl Junction, with Class 37 No 37210 at the head and No 37229 *Cardiff Rod Mill* at the rear.

In 1988 a proposal for a new two-platform station at Clydach Court was submitted by Mid Glamorgan County Council. However, it would be an expensive undertaking and, if built, would interfere with train times between Cardiff and Merthyr. In 1990 a campaign for a halt was resurrected, and, with 6,000 people living nearby, hopes were raised, but in 1991 the proposal was again rejected, especially as resources had been focused on the re-opening of the Maesteg line and the opening of a new station at Pontyclun. However, a spokesman for the County Council Transportation Department stated that the opening of a station near Glyncoch, in the Clydach Court area, would remain under review, but today, more than 13 years later, still nothing has been built. *D. G. Thomas/Author*

Above This is Stormstown Sidings, looking towards Abercynon. In the distance is the Carn Parc road bridge, which carries the road from the Clydach Court area to Abercynon village. These sidings were used for the storage of coal traffic from the nearby Lady Windsor Colliery at Ynysybwl; in the foreground is the disused and partially lifted track leading from the nearby viaduct. *Author*

Below Former GWR engine No 5601 is taking water at Carn Parc Sidings, near Abercynon, on 12 January 1960 while employed on up goods duties, as per the 'J6' target; this engine has already been here earlier in the day with empties from Stormstown Junction to the Black Lion sidings, for Merthyr Vale Colliery, and will have picked up the Abercynon banking engine, carrying target 'JP1', at this location for the climb up the valley. This is a 5600 Class engine, built at Swindon in 1924 and withdrawn in 1965. On the right is the gate over the single line that led to the NCB small coal stack siding, used in the early 1970s for coal taken to the Aberthaw Power Station. *The late S. Rickard, J and J collection*

Above Photographed from near the Carn Parc Hotel, looking down on to the track between Carn Parc and Abercynon, 5600 Class No 5691 heads a mixed train around the gentle curve as it heads up the valley on 23 September 1964. This scene is typical of this part of South Wales, with steep hilly sides full of vegetation. The smoke from the hard-pressed engine catches the sun's early rays, magically mixing with the mist rising from the valley foliage. *B. J. Ashworth*

Below Abercynon station was known as Navigation House when it opened in October 1840, and was located 50 yards further north than the present station. The new station, named Aberdare Junction, arrived with the opening of the Aberdare branch on 5 August 1846, and was renamed Abercynon on 1 December 1896. It closed to goods traffic on 20 April 1964, and became Abercynon South in October 1988 when a new station, called Abercynon North, was opened on the Aberdare branch (almost on the site of the original Navigation House). Abercynon South Station is still in use for passenger services.

This was the view of the station, photographed from the riverside, circa 1900. Abercynon North signal box is on the right; this box opened in 1897, replacing an earlier one on the same site, and was closed by the GWR on 3 March 1932. The station sign reads 'Abercynon Change For Aberdare'. *Author's collection*

Above On 3 August 1957 No 6431, with an auto-train, forms the 11.25am Abercynon to Aberdare (Low Level) service. The leading vehicle is No W111W, a converted GWR steam railcar, formerly No 13 – its slatted wooden body is quite noticeable. No 6431 spent a considerable period located in the Landore area before moving to Aberdare, where it stayed until February 1962; this 6400 Class loco was built in 1937, and withdrawn from service in 1963. *The late S. Rickard, J and J collection*

Below This view of the north end of the station on 13 July 1958, looking across the lines from the engine shed area, is very unusual. The car neatly framed under the arm of the

water pump, parked on the railway-owned approach road between the station and the shed, is a 1934 Hillman Minx, purchased by the late H. C. Casserley in 1957. 'Maggie' visited South Wales in 1958, 1959 and 1960, was laid up late in the latter year when the MOT test was introduced, and finally sold in 1970 for restoration. According to *Slaters Directory* of 1880, Aberdare Junction's Station Master at that time was Mr Joseph Hiscock, who was still in post in 1903; by 1913 Mr A. Churchill held the job. In the right foreground is the sand-drying shed, beyond which is 3700 Class No 3707, built at Swindon in 1936 and withdrawn in 1964. Today the station is still in use for passenger services only, and the shed building is still in situ, having been used by a private firm for many years, but up for sale again at the time of writing. *R. M. Casserley*

Opposite top In this bird's-eye view of the station on 23 September 1964, bottom right is Abercynon signal box. Passing the box is Pannier tank No 9611 (built in 1945 and withdrawn in 1965), acting as banker to No 5691 (built in 1927 and also withdrawn in 1965) and its heavy train of mixed wagons and vans heading north up the valley; it can be seen that it has taken the line towards Merthyr, and is about to tackle the mile-long climb at 1 in 40. The train engine is in line with the original TVR station house; to the right of it is the railway canteen, which later became the British Railways Staff Club.

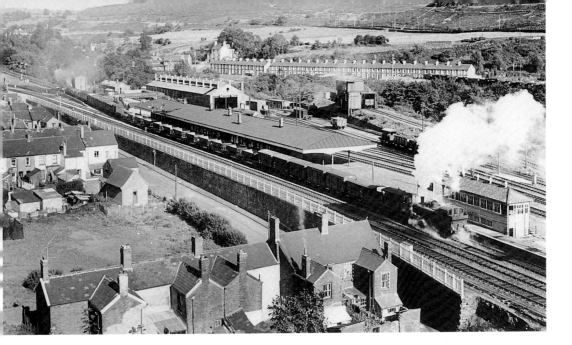

The author has spent many an hour there, in the good company of railwaymen, both former and serving, and their families, and it was a sad day when the club closed. In the left distance the Aberdare line diverges from the main line. Behind the signal box is the line that was used as a sand drag to arrest the speed of any runaway trains. In the middle distance is the coaling stage, and to its left the engine shed. Beyond them both is Martins Terrace, and well above, on the hillside, is the TVR line heading for Nelson. *B. J. Ashworth*

Middle Looking north from the down platform on 29 June 1960, the start of the incline can be seen in the left distance. At the far end of the platform a member of staff is pulling a platform trolley, one of those heavy wooden things with cast-iron wheels that never seemed to be greased! The engine shed is on the right, and there is a good view of the sand-drying building. The engine in view is No 5623, another of the numerous 5600 Class, this one built in 1923 and withdrawn in 1964. In the right background, at the end of the terraced houses, was the Dowlais Cardiff Colliery, usually known by now as the Abercynon Colliery. *R. M. Casserley*

Bottom The first engine shed at Abercynon was built by the TVR in 1853 and closed in 1928, to be replaced by this shed, built by the GWR in 1929 and closed by British Railways on 2 November 1964. It was then used to stable diesels for about 12 months, from 1986 onwards, then used by a private firm for many years. On the approach road circa 1960 is a Hillman Minx, and behind it, on the extreme left, a Morris 1000 saloon. *The late Trefor David, courtesy of C. L. Caddy*

Below On 13 July 1958 Pannier tank No 3707 stands alongside the engine shed in a photograph that captures the scene nicely and provides a better view of the shed entrance, with the sand drying shed outside. This and the other photographs of this once busy station will hopefully provide plenty of inspiration for modellers. *R. M. Casserley*

Below This interesting photograph shows several classes of engines at the Abercynon coaling stage on 5 November 1958. On the right is 3700 Class No 3730, built in 1937 and withdrawn in 1964, and to the left is No 5623, built in 1925 and withdrawn in 1964, while an unknown engine is being coaled. In front of them are some six- and nine-plank coal wagons, and in the centre is a lookout man, with a warning horn tucked under his arm, keeping a careful watch to warn the nearby permanent way gang of the danger of passing trains; one of the gangers is checking the tracks for defects. *R. S. Carpenter*

Left In the shed yard on 6 May 1951 is former TVR 'A' Class No 409, built by Hawthorn Leslie, works number 3410, in 1920. It has the taper boiler it received from the GWR in 1930, and the GWR number 398. It was withdrawn in 1957. Behind it is a carriage used by the Loco Carriage & Wagon Department at Abercynon, indicated by the sign on its roof; it is part of the depot's breakdown train, which normally consisted of two special four-wheeled vans: this is the Riding Van, still lettered 'GW', and the other is the Tool and Package Van, seen here on the extreme right. *R. M. Casserley*

Above Abercynon signal box, photographed on 19 May 1988, was opened on 3 April 1932, and originally came from Birmingham Moor Street station. Some time at the beginning of the 1970s the platform was raised, and the entrance to the signal box was relocated to this north end. Seen here is relief signalman Terry Morgan, now retired, handing the token to the driver of 'Sprinter' No 150275 giving him authority to proceed over the single line towards Merthyr. *Author*

Below The last TVR engine to haul a passenger train into Abercynon station circa 1952 was former 'A' Class No 139, built in 1919 by Nasmyth Wilson, works number 1273, reboilered in 1926, and seen here with its GWR number 373 passing the Abercynon Station Master's house on the Merthyr line. The driver is Mr William Thomas, and his fireman Mr Dennis Jones; both were based at Abercynon shed, and their engine was withdrawn from service in 1957. *Aberdare Library*

Above Looking down the 1 in 40 gradient of Abercynon Bank on 6 February 1971, work is being undertaken to remove the double track, converting the line back to single-line operation. In the background an engineering train is hard at work removing the former down line, while on the right the up line is in use for all traffic, under 'wrong line working' restrictions; the trap points have been clipped shut. The embankment on the right is part of the original rope-worked incline, the steepness of which is remarkable. *B. Morris*

Below Incline Top station, opened in 1846 and renamed Top of the Incline Station in May 1849, was closed on 1 January 1858. The station building was partially destroyed by a cyclone on 27 October 1913, a natural disaster that also caused great damage to the nearby districts of Cilfynydd, Abercynon and Quakers Yard. This photograph shows the Top of the Incline Station at Penlocks, near Abercynon, circa 1862, and the steps that passengers used to reach the bottom of the cutting and board their train. In the background is the Royal Oak Hotel. *A. G. Powell collection*

Above This is an unusual photograph of 5700 Class No 9632 acting as banking engine on an up train on 23 September 1964. Looking anxiously through the cab glass are both driver and fireman, while on the left, under the Booking Office sign is a poster stating 'Give Dad a break', but from what is your guess, as the rest of the words are too small to read! This former GWR Swindon engine was built in 1945 and withdrawn in 1964. *B. J. Ashworth*

ABERDARE JUNCTION STATION.
MAIN LINE DIVISION.

20. No Engine, or Train is to leave this Station to proceed down the Line towards Newbridge (beyond the Llancaiach Branch Junction);

On Week Days,
H.   M.
After, 8   10 morning
12   40 afternoon

Nor must any Down Goods Train leave,

On Week Days,
H.   M.
After,   7   40 morning
12   10 afternoon

Until the expiration of Ten Minutes, after the departure of the respective Down Passenger Trains from this Station;

Nor after, on Week Days, | On Sundays,
H.   M. | H.   M.
6   15 evening | 8   40 morning
                                  | 3   40 afternoon

Nor must any Down Goods Train leave,

On Week Days,
H.   M.
After,   5   45 afternoon

Until the Up Passenger Train has arrived at the foot of the Incline, after the Down Passenger Train has passed out of the Cutting; and provided that a period of Ten Minutes has elapsed since the departure of the Down Passenger Train.

21. No Engine, or Train is to leave this Station to go to the Llancaiach Branch, unless there is a clear Twenty Minutes, before the appointed time of arrival of an Up Passenger Train; and Ten Minutes before the appointed time of departure of a Down Passenger Train at this Station, until the arrival of the respective Up Passenger Trains, or until the expiration of Fifteen Minutes after the departure of the respective Down Passenger Trains (as the case may be); in such cases, it can only be allowed when the Train is sufficiently light, that the Engine will be able to shunt it easily into the Llancaiach Branch, in every respect clear, so that neither line of Rails will be in the least obstructed.

22. The Main Lines of Rails at this Station, are to be kept in every respect clear for the safe passage of the Passenger Trains; and especially the points, roads and crossings near the entrance of the cutting, by at least Fifteen Minutes, before the appointed time of arrival at this Station of the Passenger Trains, travelling in either direction.

23. No Down Engine, or Train is to leave this Station, from any of the Sidings eastward of the Main Line of Rails, on Week Days, between the departure of the last Down Passenger Train, and the arrival of the last Up Passenger Train; nor on Sundays, between the departure of the first Down Passenger Train, and the arrival of the first Up Passenger Train; or between the departure of the second Down Passenger Train, and the arrival of the second Up Passenger Train at this Station.   See Rule 362, and Section 19.

ABERDARE BRANCH DIVISION.

24. No Engine, or Train is to leave this Station to pass up the Aberdare Branch, in front of a Passenger or Mail Train, unless there is a clear Fifteen Minutes on Week Days, and Twenty Minutes on Sundays, before the appointed time of departure from this Station, of the Up Passenger or Mail Train for Aberdare, until the expiration of Ten Minutes, after the departure of the respective Up Passenger or Mail Trains from this Station, for Aberdare.

MAIN INCLINE TOP.

25. No Engine, or Train is to leave this Station, to precede an Up Passenger Train, unless there is a clear Thirty Minutes, before the appointed time for the departure of the Up Passenger Train from this Station; until the expiration of Ten Minutes, after such Up Passenger Train has left this Station for Merthyr.

26. No Engine, or Train is to leave this Station to proceed towards Merthyr,

On Week Days, | On Sundays,
H.   M. | H.   M.
After,   7   25 morning | After, 8   5 morning
11   55 morning | 3   5 afternoon
5   40 afternoon |

Until the respective Down Passenger Trains have arrived at this Station from Merthyr.

MERTHYR STATION.

27. No Engine, or Train is to leave this Station, to pass down the line towards Troedyrhiew, to precede a Passenger Train, unless there is a clear Thirty Minutes, before the appointed time of departure of such Passenger Train; until the expiration of Ten Minutes, after such Passenger Train has left this Station.

28. Whenever an Engine follows the third Down Passenger Train (No. 39), the Station Master is to send printed Instructions to the Engineman and Policeman at the Incline Top, by such third Down Passenger Train (No. 39), stating that an Engine is following that Down Passenger Train to the Incline Top, in such cases the third Up Passenger Train (No. 40), is to wait at the Incline Top, until the arrival there of the Down Goods Train.

29. No Engine, or Train is to leave this Station, to pass down the Line towards Troedyrhiew,

On Week Days, | On Sundays,
H.   M. | H.   M.
After,   9   10 morning | After 8   45 morning
2   40 afternoon | 3   45 afternoon
6   40 evening |

Until the respective Up Passenger Trains have arrived at this Station.

An extract from the TVR Working Timetable of May 1856 regarding 'Aberdare Junction'. In addition, the TVR Rule Book of the period also stated: 'The up mail vans to be the last vehicle in the train, going from the Incline Top to Merthyr.' By permission of Mrs Irene Morton Lloyd, widow of the late Mike Morton Lloyd.

The following article regarding Abercynon Bank was written for *Archive* magazine, the quarterly magazine of the Welsh Railway Research Circle, and is included by permission of Mr Colin Chapman.

In laying out the Taff Vale Railway, Brunel adopted the more direct route, but relied on contemporary practice, in the form of a rope-worked incline, to overcome the change in levels. One beneficial result of this expedient was that Brunel was able to employ relatively easy gradients on the rest of the line.

The stationary engine for this incline was delivered around the end of 1840. This Main Incline, as it was always called by the TVR, was 880 yards long and comprised two equal sections of 1 in 20¾ and 1 in 18. The establishment at the engine house consisted of two enginemen and a brake rider. The initial working arrangements were somewhat hair-raising. Trains left Cardiff and Merthyr timed so as to synchronise at the incline – as the up train approached the foot of the incline, the locomotive was detached and put on a spurt in order to be turned off the main line before the carriages reached the foot of the incline. In the case of down trains, the locomotive was removed from the train, which was then allowed to move forward, under the control of the brakesman, to the top of the incline, where the rope was attached. The down train then descended as the up train ascended. The locomotives did not work on the incline but returned to their respective originating stations with the carriages that had worked up or down.

The Main Incline appears to have been remarkably free from accident until Christmas Day 1848, when the afternoon down train arrived at the top of the incline, and its carriages were moved forward to the rope in the usual way to await the arrival of the up train at the foot of the incline.

The train was a long one (the usual formation was six vehicles) and the weight of the train caused the coupling between the ninth and tenth coaches to break, resulting in the first nine coaches enjoying the dubious privilege of an unrestrained run down the incline. Fortunately the up train had not yet arrived at the bottom, and the down train was thus able to career all the way down through Navigation station without damage to itself or injury to the passengers. Had the up train been at the foot of the incline, the consequences would doubtless have been somewhat more traumatic.

This incident exposed the inherent defects in the method of working the Main Incline, and was the subject of a lengthy report by George Fisher in March 1849.

The Taff Vale Railway Act of 1857 included powers for the replacement of the Main Incline with a locomotive incline at a gradient of 1 in 36. This did not imply early action, however, as the Act was a very far-sighted measure that included powers, such as the quadrupling of the main line, that were not exercised for many years.

In March 1864 George Fisher was able to recommend the replacement of the Main Incline with a locomotive incline, and on 18 March 1864 the Board resolved to adopt his recommendation. The new incline was built alongside the old, but with a gradient of 1 in 40 in place of the 1 in 36 shown on the Parliamentary Sections; this resulted in substantially greater earthworks. Work got off to a good start but was retarded by inclement weather in the early part of 1865, and again in the same period of 1866. In May 1867 George Fisher reported that over £29,000 had been paid to the contractor, that the rails and girders had cost £6,000, and that a further expenditure of £5,000 was required to complete the work. In August 1867 Mr Fisher was able to report that the new locomotive incline was completed.

Quakers Yard

The 1862 doubling of the line also involved Quakers Yard Viaduct No 68, where a second bridge was built alongside Brunel's 1840 original. However, colliery workings beneath the structure caused constant problems. On 3 November 1900, for example, a permanent way gang working on this part of the line reported that settlement of the abutments had occurred. As a result of these and other observations Mr Sibbering, the TVR's Engineer at Cardiff wrote to the General Manager of the Ocean Coal Company on 4 December 1901 asking for information relating to colliery workings near the viaduct; on 10 December he also wrote to the General Manager of the Taff Vale Railway, stating that owing to subsidence caused by workings from the Treharris Pit, it would be necessary for the masonry structure to be strengthened with steel girders.

The TVR Board minutes of January 1902 report that Messrs Frazer's tender for £917 was to be accepted for the work, to be paid for by the Taff Vale Railway. However, the damage had been done, subsidence was still occurring and periodical checks had be made using bench marks and the former levels to get a true picture of just how much movement there was.

By 1931 subsidence was again creating major problems, and on 3 January estimates were accepted for the shoring, repairing and securing of the viaduct using timber, the cost totalling £20,888. It was decided at a general meeting held at Cardiff on that day to ask the colliery companies for compensation, via the TVR company solicitors. Thus started some lengthy negotiations and letters. On 20 June 1931 the GWR's Civil Engineer reported:

'Quakers Yard Viaduct No 68.
Built 1840 by Brunel, as a single viaduct with splayed spans of six semi arches, 50 feet wide; viaduct widened in 1862, concentre with original arches, but of 56 feet span, width 15 feet, giving a total width of 29 feet; underside of original arches have dressed faces, down-

This photograph shows the opening up and widening of the original cutting and tunnel at Goitrecoed, near Quakers Yard, to enable double track to be laid on this previously single-track section. The contractor's engine and temporary track can be seen in this view looking towards Incline Top circa 1862. *A. G. Powell collection*

Work is under way doubling the main line and building a second viaduct alongside the original
Brunel viaduct of 1840 at Quakers Yard, circa 1862 (see page 119). *A. G. Powell collection*

side faces are rock-faced and require rendering as laggings are fixed; three centres about 6 feet 6 inches apart under up-line side, centres supported on five frames carried up from ground level over river, three girders on concrete abutments about 8 feet from normal water level, heaviest girder about 15 tons.

Coal seams average 6 feet thick and 650 yards deep, end-on approach at 70 yards per year; 330-yard-wide face 100 yards from south end of viaduct at present.

Prior to amalgamation in 1922, first seam of coal at a depth of about 550 yards was worked from under this viaduct, with a surface subsidence to 1 foot 6 inches at least.

Timbering was started in 1924 and 90 per cent completed, with 40,000 cubic feet of timber being estimated for this viaduct.

The actual amount against the colliery companies proportion came to £3,093, which was 65 per cent of materials and labour towards stabilising this viaduct, with a maximum liability payment by the collieries involved of £25,000, this sum being finalised on 23 October 1932.'

While those negotiations were taking place, a further report was presented by the mining engineers:

'16 August 1932: regards the Lady Windsor Pit, no developments likely to effect TVR main line, or the branch to Abercynon Colliery, since last report; only small areas of 4-foot seams under and near Ynysybwl Branch, about 10 chains and 12 chains north; new mining recently, by cross measure drift to Bute seam from main level outside area of protection, so many years before any development will effect railway.'

It seems that from that period little subsidence occurred – a little settling, but nothing serious – until October 1936, when once again major problems arose. On 26 July 1938 a memo was sent to Mr A. W. Hollingdale of the GWR Estate Offices, Cardiff, from Mr W. D. Johns BSc, of the Divisional Engineers Office, Queen Street, Cardiff, stating that a special and accurate system of levels had now been taken over regular intervals since 1 October 1937, when a rapid movement had first became apparent; previous taking of levels, which had been discontinued in 1934, had given little useful information, as there was then only a relatively small amount of movement by the viaduct, but in October 1936 checks had once again been carried out, causing alarm due to the increased movement; even the previously used bench marks had moved, so new readings were taken at fresh points of up to a distance of some 10 chains from the viaduct.

From 3 March 1938 these new levels were checked and noted on a regular basis, and it was recorded that subsidence had occurred to a depth of 1½ inches; checked again on 21 July 1938, more subsidence had occurred, this time to a further depth of 2¾ inches, giving a total subsidence in eight months of some 4 inches. In total the viaduct had moved between 9 and 11½ inches throughout its whole length, and on further investigation it was found that the crowns were settling in line with the piers located behind, thus putting a greater pressure on the arch and causing a lifting effect on the timber centring. Something would have to be done, as this centring was taking no weight at all; it also became apparent that the centring would have to incorporate a heavier transverse bracing in the haunch of the arch, which would give support to the arches against the larger crushing force. The report made it clear that steps would have to be taken very shortly, especially regarding the up-side parapet, although there was no apparent damage being caused to the actual arches.

The problems were again being created by mining, mainly from the Lady Windsor Colliery, Ynysybwl, the Deep Navigation Colliery, Treharris, and the Dowlais Cardiff Colliery, Abercynon. The TVR, and its successor the GWR, was not slow in taking action against the collieries concerned. During this period colliery workings were causing a great deal of trouble for the railway network in South Wales, and there was a never-ending battle against the threat of subsidence and collapse to ensure safety for rail passengers.

In the 1980s and 1990s constant checks were still being carried out on this viaduct by the Bridges Department of British Rail, in joint consultation with the Mining Engineers Department at Derby, who carried out constant monitoring of any pit workings in the area. Today the collieries have closed and in many cases the sites built upon, but Network Rail continues to carry out checks, and the trains still use the viaduct, indicating that safety standards are as good today as they were before. Meanwhile the piece of the steel centring that came away from the viaduct many years ago, and still lies embedded among the stones in the River Taff, is there to act as a reminder that safety to the public must always come first.

This is the TVR viaduct at Quakers Yard, otherwise known as Goitre Viaduct after a nearby farm, looking towards Abercynon circa 1960. On the right-hand parapet, about half way across, is a dressed stone dated '1840', and opposite it another carrying the date '1862'. A 30mph speed restriction is in force over the viaduct. On the door of the permanent way cabin are inscribed the figures '18' and '14', indicating miles and chains. *S. Fisher*

Above A 1930s postcard view of Quakers Yard and the Taff Valley. The viaduct on the extreme left is on the GWR & Rhymney Joint line, taking it over the Taff towards Merthyr Tydfil via Abercanaid. To its right is the Vale of Neath viaduct, more properly known as the Taff Vale Extension Railway viaduct, carrying that line over the river and through a tunnel towards Aberdare, where it becomes the Vale of Neath Railway. Both viaducts have been strengthened due to mining subsidence. In the centre is a train of coal wagons that will pass beneath both lines on the Taff Vale Railway en route to Merthyr Tydfil, following the course of the river instead of crossing it. In the right middle distance is the TVR's Quakers Yard (Low Level) station, and above it the High Level station; between them are exchange sidings. On the right is the TVR's Quakers Yard Viaduct over the Taff River, also timber-strengthened due to mining subsidence. In the far distance is the mining village of Treharris, with its station on the Taff Vale Extension line. *Author's collection*

Left The TVR's Quakers Yard Low Level station opened in January 1858, and had exchange sidings with the High Level Station, which had opened a year earlier. Today all traces of the latter and the exchange sidings have been erased by a new housing complex, but the former TVR station is still in use for passengers, albeit modernised with a modern 'bus stop'-type shelter. Looking towards Merthyr, this is a good general view of the station from the exchange sidings on 15 July 1959. *R. M. Casserley*

Top The down-side waiting room is seen here from an unusual angle, looking down from the High Level station, on 15 July 1959. The architecture of the building is shown to good effect. *R. M. Casserley*

Middle Former GWR Pannier tank No 3734 (built in 1937 and withdrawn in 1964) runs light through the station on 27 September 1960. In the background can be seen the TVR-designed signal box, which closed in 1965, while on the left, and just in view, is the morning school train, providing memories of the 1960s with duffle coats and satchels in abundance! In the top right-hand corner is the rear of the High Level station. *R. M. Casserley*

Bottom The Low Level station is seen here looking towards Incline Top in June 1921. The exchange sidings are seen here on the left, and in the foreground is a gas lamp characteristic of the period, which, when lit by the station night staff, gave off a warming yellow glow. *The late S. Rickard, J and J collection*

Merthyr

Above This October 1987 panorama shows the rear view of the BR-designed Black Lion signal box (see page 83), which was originally on the Llanelli to Cynheidre branch. Seen from the opposite side of the Taff River, this view also shows the sidings and some BR HAA coal hoppers for the nearby Merthyr Vale Colliery. On the extreme right, where the trees are, was the site of the viaduct that carried Rhymney traffic from the Abercanaid branch, at Merthyr Vale Junction, over the river to these sidings, which were officially known as Rhymney Sidings. The concrete foundations for the bridge pillars, which is all that is left of the viaduct, can still be seen with difficulty. Black Lion

signal box closed on 21 June 1992, and at the same time the sidings were lifted. The road running between the houses and signal box is named Tram Road, and is built on the former Trevithick tramway, or Penydarren Tramroad, as it is also known. *Author*

Below The shaft at Merthyr Vale Colliery was sunk in 1869, and opened for production in 1875. Originally part of the Nixons Navigational Steam Coal Company, in the 1930s ownership passed to the Powell Duffryn Group. This November 1984 photograph shows a busy colliery scene with a British Rail 08 Class diesel shunter hard at work shunting coal wagons on somewhat dubious internal rails. The colliery closed in 1989. *Author*

Top Merthyr Vale station opened on 1 June 1883, with goods facilities starting in 1885. It closed to goods traffic on 25 February 1957, but remains in use today for passenger services. This circa 1910 view is looking down the line towards Quakers Yard, showing the path leading down from the bridge to the up-side waiting room and platform. Note the lantern-type gas lamps, used on most TVR stations for many years. *J. Morris*

Middle Looking in the opposite direction from platform level circa 1960, the former 'swan-neck' gas lamps are now electrically operated and look rather graceful ranged along the platform. The building on the left is the up-side waiting room and gentlemen's toilet, and on the right is the down-side waiting room, with the booking office above at road level. The corrugated tin shelter stands on the site of the former signal box, and the large building next to the bridge is the rear end of a chapel. The road crossing the line goes from the main Cardiff Road over the colliery level crossing to the colliery entrance. Today only the up platform is in use for trains in both directions, with the down platform gradually returning to nature. The Victorian buildings were dismantled in 1972 and replaced with a new brick shelter on the up side. *Lens of Sutton Collection*

Bottom Troedyrhiw station (originally 'Troed yr hiew') opened on 12 April 1841 and closed to goods traffic on 7 October 1963, but is still in use for passenger services. This 1960s photograph, facing down the valley, gives a good view of the buildings and footbridge, while grandfather, father and son await a down train. Today a single line on the up side and a brick-built waiting shelter has replaced all this. *Lens of Sutton Collection*

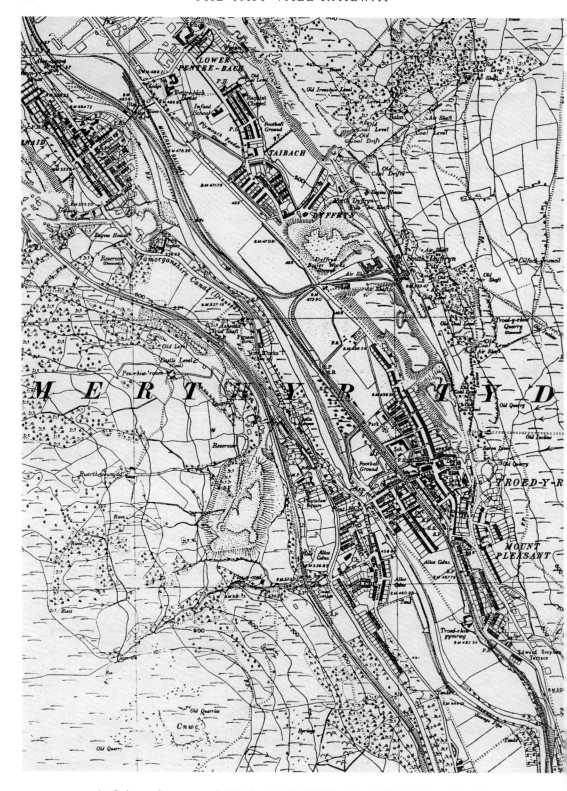

An Ordnance Survey map of 1948 showing the TVR line through Troedyrhiw on the right of the river and canal, and the Great Western & Rhymney Joint line on the left. *Crown copyright*

A permanent way gang carry out their work near Pentrebach on 6 February 1971 during the singling of this main line. They are slewing the line over to join the other one, getting the levels right and removing the redundant line. B. Morris

On 25 January 1971 Mr E. R. Williams, Divisional Manager for British Rail, Western Region, issued the following directive, Notice No W.W353:

'Between the hours of 22.00 Saturday, 6th February, and 1800, Sunday, 7th February 1971, or until completion of work, the Chief Signal and Telecommunications Engineer, and the Divisional Civil Engineer, will be carrying out the following work.

The existing double line between Black Lion and Merthyr will become single line, the down line between Merthyr Station and the Abercynon end of Pentrebach Platform, and the up line from the above latter point to Black Lion, will be used as the single line. At Black Lion a new signal box, to replace the existing signal box, will be brought into use, 10 yards on the Abercynon side of the existing signal box. The existing up main home bracket signal will be repositioned on the same side of the line, 341 yards from the signal box, with no alteration to height or form; the existing down main distant signal will apply to the new single line, new ground signals will be brought into use, all existing signals other than those will be recovered, and the existing double-line section, Black Lion to Merthyr, will become a single-line section worked under the "No Signalman Key Token" system.

The up main starting signal and the loop siding starting signal to Merthyr will be released by token withdrawn, effective for "one pull only", the down main starting signal, together with the ground discs routed from the colliery sidings and loop sidings to the down main, will be released by token withdrawn, with a similar "one pull" feature, and in addition a new auxiliary token instrument will be provided on the Black Lion-Merthyr section at a hut adjacent to the up main starting bracket signal.

A telephone to Black Lion signal box will be provided from the new auxiliary token hut, and the up intermediate block signal between Black Lion and Merthyr, together with its associated telephone will be recovered.'

Top Pentrebach station opened on 1 August 1886 and is still in use today. This photograph, circa 1900, shows the station as seen from the bank of the Taff River, from the Abercanaid side; the river is on a bend at this point, with a shale bank near the photographer. The footbridge allows pedestrians to cross over from Cardiff Street, Abercanaid village, to reach the station, or continue to Cardiff Road, Lower Pentrebach. The station nameboard reads 'Pentrebach for Abercanaid', and the building nearest camera is the up-side booking office and waiting room. The building with the vented roof is the gentlemen's toilet, a very typical TVR style of building. *Lens of Sutton Collection*

Middle Pentrebach station is seen circa 1958 from the down platform looking towards Troedyrhiw. The down-side toilet building is almost hidden by the foliage, but there is a good view of the gentlemen's toilet and waiting room on the up side. *Lens of Sutton Collection*

Bottom This is the down-side waiting room on 10 August 1968 – the gentlemen's toilet is at this end, while the doors for the ladies' toilet and waiting room are on the front. It is built of Blue Pennant stonework edged with yellow engineering brick. *D. G. Thomas*

The original Taff Vale Railway station at Merthyr opened on 12 April 1841; situated just south of the town, it was known as Plymouth Street Station. When the Vale of Neath Railway, also engineered by Brunel, opened its own station at Merthyr, called High Street, on 2 November 1853, its approach passed over the TVR line just south of Plymouth Street by way of a long viaduct.

On 1 August 1877 the TVR and GWR opened a joint line from Brandy Bridge on the former to Mardy Junction on the latter, which was advantageous to both companies. A year later, on 1 August 1878, the TVR transferred its passenger services to High Street, and Plymouth Street became a goods depot only; the GWR named it Merthyr Plymouth Street in July 1924. This goods depot and the junction signal box closed on 27

November 1967 and 1968 respectively, and after closure the depot was taken over by National Carriers Ltd, then by British Telecom; today it is covered by an Aldi superstore complex.

A branch from Dowlais Junction to Dowlais Iron Works station opened for goods and passenger traffic on 2 August 1851. Passengers were carried for a total of only three years, until May 1854, although general freight was carried until 1876; mineral traffic was carried until closure of the Dowlais Iron Works in October 1930, and the track was removed in 1945.

The Ynysfach branch to the nearby Cyfarthfa Ironworks was officially closed on 23 March 1950, but a short section of 6 chains was used for shunting purposes by Plymouth Street Goods Depot.

Brandy Bridge Junction is seen on 4 April 1955. The line on the extreme left leads towards the river bridge, various railway vans occupy the sidings, and the engine (ex-GWR 5700 Class No 7766, built by the North British Locomotive Co in 1931, works number 24054, and withdrawn in 1960) is on the one of the lines that led to the original TVR station at Plymouth Street. When TVR passenger services commenced from High Street station in 1878, Plymouth Street became a goods depot. The line to the right of the engine passes beneath the line to High Street, which marks the start of the incline to Dowlais Iron Works and is known as Dowlais Junction, while the High Street line itself from Brandy Bridge carries the former TVR up to and across the GWR-built viaduct that leads to Merthyr High Street station. In the background can be seen the former Vale of Neath viaduct. The signal box was built by the TVR, opened in 1889 and closed on 27 November 1967. M. Hale

Top A 5-ton second-hand tramcar is being taken from Plymouth Street Goods Depot to the Electric Depot, with help from a five-horse hitch, circa 1930. The goods agent at Plymouth Street in 1892 was Mr Clay, and from 1903 until at least 1913 it was Mr W. Thompson. *Merthyr Tydfil Public Library*

Middle Delivery drays are lined up at the TVR goods platform at Plymouth Street circa 1930. Carts like these were used by all railway companies for many years – in 1928 the GWR had more than 4,000 horse-drawn carts like these in regular use around its system, until finally replaced by the petrol-driven Scarab 'mechanical horse' three-wheel tractor and trailer. *Merthyr Tydfil Public Library*

Bottom This TVR postcard shows 0-6-2T No 86, with its driver, fireman, a guard and a shunter at Plymouth Street circa 1910; this engine was a member of the 'M1' Class, built by Kitson & Co in 1891, works number 3205, and renumbered by the GWR as 481. In the background is the jointly used viaduct. *S. Fisher collection*

Railway Station, Merthyr Tydfil

JV 61316

Above Merthyr High Street was an important station shared by several railway companies, which, prior to the Grouping of 1923, when many became part of the Great Western Railway, included the Vale of Neath Railway (which arrived on 2 November 1853), the London & North Western Railway (1 June 1868), the Brecon & Merthyr Railway (1 August 1868), the Taff Vale Railway (1 August 1877), the Great Western Railway (also 1 August 1877), and the Rhymney Railway (1 April 1886).

This postcard gives a good overall view of the joint station circa 1910. On the extreme left a TVR engine is running round its train, while over on the right is the goods yard. The large building was a granary, and next to it an LNWR tank engine is about to depart with a close-coupled set of four-wheelers. The conical water tower can be seen, and to its right are some loose LNWR coaches, two 3rd Class and one Composite. The photograph was probably taken near Masonic Street. The granary was burned down by vandals in the 1990s. *Lens of Sutton Collection*

Below In this general view, circa 1930, three passenger workings are at the platforms. The photograph also shows quite well the very narrow width of the centre platform, numbered 2 and 3, especially when compared to the comparative vastness of the platforms at either side. *Lens of Sutton Collection*

Top On 25 July 1922 TVR 'A' Class engine No 414 is ready to depart with a down-valley passenger service consisting of the high-roofed stock built by Cravens in 1921. The 3rd Class and Composite coaches were 64 feet long and lasted right into the late 1950s. No 414 was built in 1921 at the Vulcan Foundry to works number 3496, reboilered by the GWR with a taper boiler in 1928 and renumbered 306, and withdrawn from service in 1956. *R. S. Carpenter*

Middle TVR engine No 75 is photographed in 1922 as the first TVR train to be lined out in the new GWR livery. Whether this is a sad moment or a proud one, especially for the driver or fireman, is hard to imagine, but one thing is certain – it will catch the eye of everyone over the next week or so. An 'A' Class locomotive from the Vulcan Foundry, it was built in 1921, works number 3492, reboilered by the GWR with a taper boiler in 1927, was renumbered 347 and withdrawn in 1956. The narrow central platform is built from timber rather than stone – originally this Vale of Neath station was broad gauge, and when re-laid as standard gauge this extra platform was squeezed in. *LCGB, Ken Nunn Collection*

Opposite bottom By August 1974 a new booking office and station building had replaced the Victorian facade, and this August 1985 view shows former GWR platform seats alongside British Railways Western Region examples, while over on the right, next to the now disused goods yard, Post Office Sherpa vans are parked. There is just one line on each side of the platform, leading to the now singled line down the valley; the rest has all been lifted except for two lines running into the goods yard, both rusty and covered with weeds, while the shunters cabins and goods shed in the yard shows nothing but dereliction.

In December 1989 the station yard was put up for tender by the British Rail Property Board; planning consent for 180,000 square feet had already been obtained, which did not include the station yard site. In 1996 the Retail Development Opportunity people closed in, and a supermarket with car park was planned, which would cover the station and adjoining yard area, while a new housing complex was to be built on the former engine shed site. A new station would be relocated a little way south of this one, at a cost of £¼ million. Thus by March 1996 demolition of the 1974 British Rail station was complete, and the new station was finished and open for passenger services by May. *Author*

Above A pair of 5700 Class Pannier tanks occupy a corner of the station yard on 11 September 1955; No 9638 was built in 1946 and withdrawn in 1963. Behind it can just be glimpsed a British Railways 'Hybar' 13-ton wagon; these had a tarpaulin rail that, when not in use, was folded down to one side. Alongside it is one of the former RCH seven-plank open coal wagons, and in front of that a British Railways 12-ton open steel mineral wagon of the type built in the early 1950s to an LNER design. *R. M. Casserley*

Below For many years Merthyr (High Street) Station Yard was a very busy place, but in November 1984 it is a scene of neglect and abandonment. Today it is part of a new Tesco superstore complex. *Author*

Top The first engine shed at Merthyr was that of the Vale of Neath Railway, built in 1854. The GWR rebuilt the shed in 1877, and in 1932 the three road building was re-roofed and lengthened. This postcard view is dated Saturday 16 April 1927, and shows the GWR shed of 1877. In the background is a GKN wagon, some LMS vans and an LMS brake-van, while over on the left a young boy leans against the telegraph post and watches the GWR engines simmering outside their shed. *C. W. Harris collection*

Middle This view shows the GWR sheds of 1932 in about 1960. There is at least one engine inside, and on the right is 5600 Class No 5699 outside the coaling shed. On the extreme right is a British Railways 16-ton mineral wagon of the welded steel type next to an older wooden-planked one. No 5699 was built in 1927, and withdrawn from service in 1964. *The late Trefor David, courtesy of C. L. Caddy collection*

Bottom A close-up of 0-6-2T No 5699 outside the coaling shed. It looks as though it has dropped its fire and the firebox has been raked clean. Outside are the fire irons, a long-handled shovel and poker. Between the engine and the shed is a mineral wagon from the East Midland Division of British Railways. The shed closed in November 1964, and today a new housing complex covers the area, with no trace left of what once was. *The late Trefor David, courtesy of C. L. Caddy collection*

2. BUTE WEST AND EAST DOCKS, CARDIFF

The Taff Vale Railway originally used only the West and East Docks via its East Docks Branch, but a later addition was the Roath Dock, which opened to traffic in 1888, and in 1907 the Alexandra Dock, all part of the Marquess of Bute Docks at Cardiff. Although used extensively by the TVR, these docks were only leased to them by the Marquess of Bute, and this, together with the ever-increasing congestion of the coal traffic en route to and at the docks meant that a solution had to be found – this was the building of the Taff Vale Railway's own dock at Penarth, and the use of the River Ely, and it was from these docks and others that the South Wales collieries sent their coal all over the world.

The July 1898 edition of *The Railway Magazine* featured an interview with Mr Ammon Beasley, TVR General Manager, who was asked by the editor, Mr G. A. Sekon, for some information covering the early difficulties – parliamentary, engineering and others – that the pioneers of Wales's earliest railway had to overcome. Beasley replied:

'…the scheme was well backed by men of capital and influence, among whom I may mention Mr (later Sir) John Josiah Guest, who was one of the first to realise that railway communication was essential to the development of the district, and was hardly the man to allow any difficulties, whether physical or financial, to stand in his way. On the contrary, the monetary difficulties were both severe and prolonged, but its subsequent success as a dividend-earning concern was so exceptional that one is apt to forget that, in most instances, they who risked their money in making the railway were not the people who made money out of it. Taff Vale stock has been as low as 22 per cent, and as high as 300.

The original Taff Vale main line extended from Merthyr to Cardiff. The scheme also included a branch to Cogan Pill, on the site of the present Penarth Dock, but that was abandoned by agreement with the late Marquess of Bute, Lord Bute, who owned

This photograph was issued to German Luftwaffe bomber crews for raids on 30 November 1941 over Cardiff's docks and elsewhere in South Wales. The line in the foreground in the GWR's South Wales main line, looking east, and the girder bridge carries the GWR spur connecting the GWR's High Street (now Central) station with the TVR lines from the docks, carried by the bridges beyond the GWR one. It shows just how important all these lines were to the war effort – damage here would have created major problems. The photograph was taken prior to 1926, as these semaphore signals were replaced in that year with electric lights. The board standing high above the lines reads 'Welsh Cold Stores'. *Pontypridd Library*

large tracts of property in Glamorganshire, got powers in 1830 to construct a dock or Ship Canal, as it was called, at Cardiff, these powers being extended in 1834.

In 1835 the Taff Vale line was projected and in 1836 was, as we have seen, sanctioned by parliament, then the Marquess of Bute, being assured of a railway to feed his dock, exercised his powers and the construction of the railway and the dock proceeded

Left Taken high above Queen Street station in January 1987, looking towards Bute Road, this photograph shows Guildford Street railway bridge and, in the right distance, Adam Street railway bridge. In the left background can be seen the area of water forming East Dock; the large prominent building near the right-hand corner is the former Spillers grain warehouse, and to the right of that is the filled-in area of West Dock. On the right-hand horizon is the landmark of Penarth Head. Today all the dockland area seen here is part of the Cardiff Bay development complex. *D. Miller*

simultaneously. Naturally Lord Bute did not like the branch to Cogan, where coal could be shipped, which might otherwise have come to his dock, so he persuaded the Taff Vale Board of Directors to abandon it in exchange for a lease of 250 years of a large part of the eastern side of his dock, now known as the West Dock, and on this land they constructed the necessary appliances for shipping coal, with a branch leading thereto. These appliances cost the Taff Vale Railway Company over £100,000, and the lease has entailed a loss upon them of some £8,000 or £9,000 every year since, while the arrangement has been very profitable to Lord Bute...

After the West Dock at Cardiff ... was

constructed, the Marquess of Bute proceeded to construct what is now known as the East Dock and that was practically completed when the Penarth Dock was projected, although the Taff Vale themselves only own Penarth Dock and Ely Harbour. The Bute Docks at Cardiff now number four, the West and East Docks already mentioned, and the Roath Dock and Roath Basin, which although called and used as a Basin, is a dock of 12 acres. There is besides another dock, authorised in 1894, which may be said to be under construction, although nothing yet has been done beyond the formation of the embankment within which the dock is to be constructed.'

Below left Photographed between the clouds in the mid-1950s, on the right is West Dock, and in the centre East Dock. At the mouth of this dock is the unique Pierhead building, the former headquarters of the Cardiff Railway. Today there are plans to use this building for the National Assembly for Wales. *Rhondda Cynon Taff County Library Service*

Below Taff Vale Railway District Map of 1910, corresponding with the photograph opposite. *A. G. Powell*

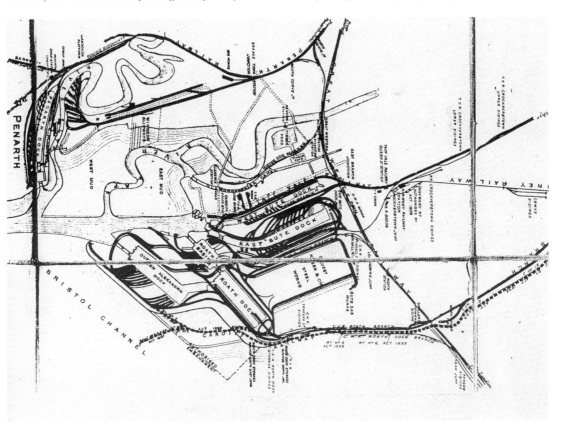

Bute West Dock

Opened in 1839, this dock was leased by the Marquess of Bute and used by the TVR on the opening of its main line on 8 August 1840. The dock closed in 1964 and subsequently was filled in. Today it is part of the modern Cardiff Bay complex, and no trace remains of this or the lines that went to it.

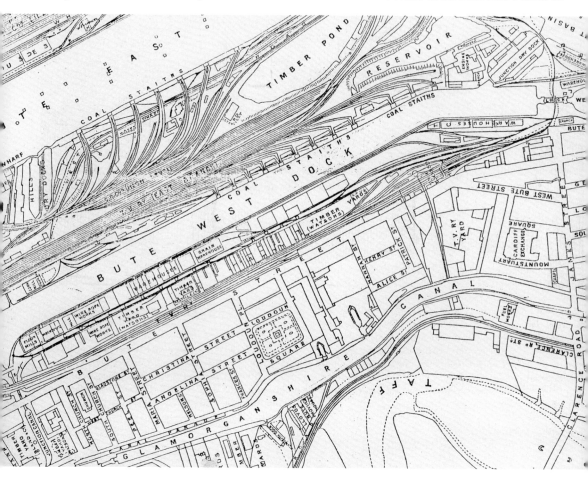

Cardiff Railway Company map of 1913, showing Bute West Dock. *Author's collection*

TVR engine *Newbridge* was built in 1846 by Messrs Benjamin Hick & Co, and is seen here at the Bute West Dock. It is thanks to the descendants of the TVR company policeman, Police Constable John Wallbridge, seen standing alongside the engine, that this unique photograph, believed to have been taken in 1850, has remained intact over the years. *Courtesy of Mr E. R. Baker OBE, South Wales Police Museum, Bridgend*

Above No 12 tip at West Dock was photographed from the vessel SS *Jacinth* at 1.25pm on 24 April 1884. To the right are some unidentifiable private owner coal wagons. This is a balance tip: chains were attached to the rear of the coal wagon, holding it securely in place while the chute and wagon tipped downwards, releasing the coal via the end doors down the tip chute and into the hold of the vessel below. *Associated British Ports*

Below These fishing trawlers were photographed in Bute West Dock in 1949, looking north. In view are the *Yasima*, *Nodzu*, *Muroto*, *Hirose*, *Hatsuse*, *Naniwa*, *Oku*, *Akita* and *Sasebo*, all with Cardiff as their port of registration. In the background, behind the *Akita*, is the spire of the Norwegian Chapel. *Associated British Ports*

Bute East Dock

The excavation work on the first part of this dock started in the early part of 1852, and it opened in July 1855, with a length of 1,000 feet and a width of 300 feet. Once the first part was completed, in the same year the engineers, Messrs Walker, Burgess & Cooper, started work on the first part of the extension, which was completed and opened in 1857; the length was now 2,000 feet and the width 500 feet. The final extension was started in 1857, and when this was completed the length had grown to 2,300 feet. The dock was finally opened completely on 1 September 1859.

Again, the dock was leased by the Marquess of Bute to the TVR, which used the coal tips on the west side, and had sidings to hold a capacity of 872 wagons. Bute East Dock closed in 1970, and today it has a closed-in waterfront, being very much a part of the Cardiff Bay development plan. Some warehouses have been completely modernised and made into flats and apartments, while the remainder were bulldozed away. Indeed, everything that was here before as part of the environment of a working dock has been swept away.

Above East Basin Tip was photographed at 12.30pm on 24 April 1884. The vessel at berth is the SS *Alchester*, which has just arrived in port. As can be seen, a great number of dockers are waiting to unload her cargo. *Associated British Ports*

Below This is No 4 tip, located on the west side of East Dock, photographed from the deck of the SS *Corinth* at 3pm on 19 April 1884. In the background can be seen the West Dock. *Associated British Ports*

Above No 2 tip at East Dock was also photographed from a ship, at 3pm on 22 April 1884, with plenty of coal wagons waiting on the approach roads to be tipped. *Associated British Ports*

Right A TVR wagon label. *L. D. Bryant*

Below Another view of No 2 tip, photographed two days later. On the left is an empty wagon from Fernhill Collieries, No 286, and next to it is a Cory Brothers Company coal wagon, No 217. On the right a small vessel is wedged between two larger ones – this is a collier, and would take its cargo of Welsh coal to ports as far away from here as London. *Associated British Ports*

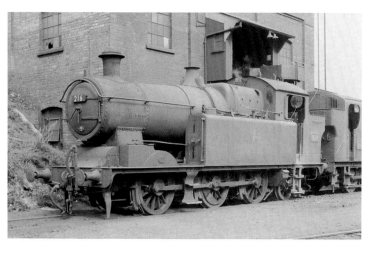

Top Former TVR 'O3' Class No 47 is seen at Cardiff East Dock engine sheds, with its GWR number 416, on 26 May 1929. Built by Hudswell Clarke in 1902, works number 582, it was withdrawn in 1932. Next to this engine is a GWR three-plank open wagon, and behind it a 20-ton GWR 'Toad' brake-van. Beyond the engine is a North Eastern wooden-planked open wagon. The East Docks engine sheds were originally used by the Rhymney Railway. *The late W. G. Boyden collection, courtesy of F. T. Hornby*

Middle At Cardiff East Docks coaling stage on 15 April 1954 is former TVR 'O4' Class No 113, carrying its GWR number 208. It was built by Beyer Peacock in 1910, works number 5387, reboilered by the GWR in 1928 with a taper boiler, and withdrawn from service in 1955. *F. T. Hornby*

Bottom Another 'O4', No 119, is seen at the coaling stage on 14 August 1954 – note the round-topped side tanks. Also built by Beyer Peacock in 1910, to works number 5392, it was reboilered by the GWR in 1940 with a taper boiler and renumbered 216, and withdrawn in 1955, scarcely a year after being photographed. *F. T. Hornby*

3. RAILWAY STAFF

This photograph was taken during the 1907 rebuilding of Pontypridd station, and shows TVR company officials, and others, visiting this busy place to see for themselves the renovations that were under way, circa 1910. Standing directly in front of the steel upright with the lettering on it, and holding an umbrella, is Mr Ammon Beasley, TVR General Manager. To his left, also holding an umbrella and wearing a bowler hat, is the Marquess of Bute; next to him is an unidentified official, then Mr A. Giles, TVR Chairman. *J. Dore-Dennis collection*

OFFICERS OF THE COMPANY.

A. BEASLEY. General Manager, Cardiff.

T. A. WALKER, Secretary, Cardiff.

G. T. SIBBERING, Engineer, Cardiff.

J. CAMERON, Locomotive Engineer, West Yard, Cardiff.

T. E. HEYWOOD, Assistant Locomotive Engineer, West Yard, Cardiff.

P. A. COLLINS, Goods Manager, Cardiff.

T. E HARLAND, Superintendent of the Line, Cardiff.

W. J BENNETT, Accountant, Cardiff.

H. SMITH, Audit Accountant, Cardiff.

S. THOMAS, Dock Superintendent, Penarth.

H. JOHNSON, Store-keeper, Cardiff Docks.

E. W. JOSCELYNE, M.D., Medical Officer, Cardiff.

CHIEF OFFICES:—CARDIFF (QUEEN STREET).

National Telephone, Nos. 2580, 2581.

STATION MASTERS AND GOODS AGENTS AT PRINCIPAL STATIONS AND DEPOTS.

ABERDARE	D. WALTERS.
ABERCYNON	A. CHURCHILL.
CARDIFF DOCKS	*H. E. SCHMUTZ.
CARDIFF (Queen St.)	S. GATHERIDGE.
CARDIFF (Queen St.)	*H. THOMAS.
COWBRIDGE	E. WILLIAMS.
CROSS INN	W. P. GLASTONBURY
FERNDALE	F. A. LOWE.
LLANTRISANT	*M. J. MORGAN.
MERTHYR	*W. THOMPSON.
MOUNTAIN ASH	W. R. DAVIES.
PENARTH DOCK AND HARBOUR	F. LUEN.
PENARTH TOWN	D. PARKER.
PONTYPRIDD	O. HURFORD.
PONTYPRIDD	*A. WILLIAMS.
PORTH	W. GIBBON.
TAFFS WELL	W. C. JOHN.
TONYPANDY AND TREALAW	R. J. MEADOWS.
TREHERBERT	W. H. VENN.
TREORCHY	R. H. CARPENTER.
YSTRAD	W. BEVAN.

*Goods Agents only.

All communications respecting Goods Rates, and the conduct of the Goods Traffic should be addressed to the Goods Manager, T.V.R., Cardiff.

Information as to Trains, Fares, and other arrangements, with respect to Passenger and Parcels Traffic may be obtained from the Superintendent of the Line, T.V.R., Cardiff

A. BEASLEY,

General Manager

Above Extract from a TVR Timetable booklet, dated 1 October 1913. *Cardiff Libraries and Information Services*

Opposite top left Mr Ammon Beasley, General Manager, Taff Vale Railway. *From The Railway Magazine, 1899*

Opposite top right Mr Tom Hurry Riches, Locomotive, Carriage & Wagon Superintendent, Taff Vale Railway. *From The Railway Magazine, 1899*

Opposite bottom left Mr T. A. Walker, Secretary, Taff Vale Railway. He began his railway career with the GWR at the age of 15. In 1890 he joined the TVR as Chief Clerk to Mr John Jones, then Goods Manager and Secretary, and continued to occupy that position under Mr Jones and his successor as Goods Manager, Mr James Tilley. In 1907, when Mr Tilley retired, Mr Walker was appointed as the new Goods Manager and remained in that position until chosen by the TVR Board of Directors to be Secretary to the company on 10 January 1913. *From The Railway Magazine, January 1913*

Opposite bottom right Mr P. A. Collins, Goods Manager, Taff Vale Railway. Mr Collins joined the TVR in 1883, as Assistant Goods Clerk at the Penarth Town station, remaining there for two years before transferring to the Traffic Manager's office. After eight years he accepted a position in the Goods Manager's office, becoming Chief Clerk in 1911. *From The Railway Magazine, January 1913*

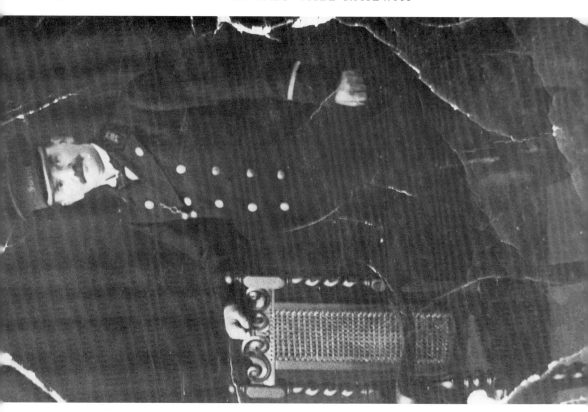

Above Mr Peter Williams (left), Penarth Town Station Master, and (right) Mr John White, both looking very smart in their TVR uniforms, circa 1910. *Mrs Lewis (née White)*

Right Mr John White was born in 1874, a local lad from the village of Treherbert, and was passenger guard on the ill-fated day when his train ran into a stationary coal train at the Gyfeillon Coke Works at Trehafod at 9.45am on 23 January 1911, suffering a broken leg. He was from a long-established railway family, and is seen here in the uniform of a guard with the newly reconstituted Great Western Railway, circa 1923. *Mrs Lewis (née White)*

Above The Quicks of Treforest were another long-established railway family, and this circa 1880 photograph shows four members dressed in the dark green corduroy uniforms of the TVR and employed as porters, together with two members dressed in the TVR blue cloth uniform of ticket collectors; this was an identical style to that worn by the GWR at the time. All are wearing the kepi style of cap with the white metal 'TVR' badge. On the extreme right the porter is wearing embroidered sleeve badges; these were first aid badges, earned by those who attended the rigorous training lessons and passed their first aid exam, and consisted of a circle of green with red edging and the letters 'TVR' over their number in the centre of the badge. *J. W. Griffiths*

Above right Mr Ted Quick, with his horse and TVR Co cart, is seen here outside The Boot and Shoe Exchange in Market Square, Pontypridd, circa 1906. *Pontypridd Library*

Right Testimonials on the retirement of 'Johnny' Quick, from the Pontypridd Observer, 22 October 1921. *Pontypridd Library*

PRESENTATION TO MR. J. QUICK.

For about fifty years Mr. "Johnny" Quick has been associated with Pontypridd Station and he has now retired. There never was a better man both for the Company and the passengers, and his friends met at the Pontypridd Station on Tuesday to make him a presentation.

Mr. J. W. John, J.P., who presided, paid a tribute to Mr. and Mrs. Quick. He said their lives were beautiful lives and were an acquisition and an asset to the town. He thought some recognition should be made and he was surprised at the ready response when he mentioned the matter. There had been six stationmasters at Pontypridd Station, Mr. Strong, Mr. Stevens, Mr. Darch, Mr. Leyshon, Mr. Felton, and their respected veteran, Mr. Hurford. (Cheers). They were presenting Mr. Quick with a walking stick as a small token of their respect and esteem. He knew of no man in Pontypridd who had lived a better life than Mr. Quick. He hoped his last days would be happy and peaceable ones. He believed that every flag on the old platform of the station was dear to him.

Mr. J. H. Davies said Mr. and Mrs. Quick were ornaments to the town. They had brought up a large family and should be proud of them. He trusted that the remaining days of Mr. and Mrs. Quick would be happy and pleasant.

Mr. Tom Pollock, in handing over the stick said he had known Mr. Quick for 24 years and he could assure him that the members of the trade he represented appreciated his efforts on their behalf and he thanked him for the courtesy extended to them from time to time.

Councillor J. T. Rees said he had known Mr. and Mrs. Quick for many years. Mr. Quick had been an honest man to the Company and an honest man to himself and if they had more like him there would be a different complexion on our country to-day. He had great pleasure in handing over the handbag to Mrs. Quick.

Mr. Hurford said they must not look at the intrinsic value of the gifts but at the good feeling that prompted them. He was sorry to lose Mr. Quick and he kept back his resignation for several months. He never came across a more loyal faithful and diligent man than Mr. Quick. (Cheers).

Mr. A. Williams also added a few words.

Inspector Johnson said he had worked 40 years with Mr. Quick and they had always been the best of friends.

Mr. John Quick, in responding said the presentation was a great surprise to him. He would take great care of the stick and hand it down to his boys and he hoped they would always look upon their dad as a man who had always done his duty.

Mrs. Quick also briefly responded.

The stick was inscribed: "Presented to John Quick, by a few Friends."

Left Mr Cliff Winstone, ticket collector at Penarth Town station, is captured in this Jerome postcard photograph, dated 28 June 1929. These postcards were popular for many years, especially as they could be posted to friends or relatives, as you would do with a ordinary postcard. *Mr F. Winstone*

Below Penarth Town station staff, both retired and serving (when this photograph was taken, circa 1960): the gentleman standing on the right was a booking office clerk, and sitting (left to right) are Alf Fry, Cliff Winstone, Mrs Winstone (station canteen lady), and two unknown gentlemen. *Mr F. Winstone*

Opposite top The first contingent of Cowbridge Volunteers, having enlisted to serve in the Great War of 1914-1918, pose at Cowbridge station on 1 September 1914. Mr Jack Bishop is among them, standing fourth from the left. *Mr G. Punter*

Opposite middle left During the 1940s two porters were employed at Cowbridge station, one in the mornings and the other for afternoons. Here are Jack Bishop (left) and Bert at midday, the change-over period, circa 1940. *The family of the late V. Bishop*

Opposite far right Miss Davies, booking office clerk at Cowbridge station in the 1930s. *The family of the late Mr V. Bishop*

Opposite bottom left Mr Daniel Punter and his dog pose in the allotments of Cowbridge station, circa 1946. *G. Punter*

Above Merthyr station staff, circa 1922, photographed in their headgear. A similar photograph was taken with everyone bare-headed! *B. Morris*

Below Merthyr station GWR Ambulance Class of 1913. Left to right, they are: back row, W. G. Hutchings, W. A. W. Jennings, A. E. Mundy and F. Hughes; middle row, E. Passmore, F. Lawrence, M. Brien, J. Graham, J. R. Boywes, R. Drew, T. J. Harries, and W. J. Shepland; front row, Sergeant H. Brown (Hon Sec and Assistant Instructor), G. Jones (President), Doctor W. W. Jones MD (Lecturer), Supt D. Davies (Instructor) and A. James (Treasurer). *B. Morris*

Above Ynysybwl station staff, circa 1915. *Mr I. Jones*

Below Guard Mr William (Billy) Lloyd (left) and Miss Joan Symonds, booking office clerk, pose beside engine No 5676; the driver is Mr Alf James. The reason for the celebrations at Pontypridd station on 8 May 1945 is VE Day, the end of the war in Europe, and less than a year before the Japanese surrender. *The Great Western Railway Magazine* of June 1945 reported the impromptu celebrations, with 0-6-2T No 5676 of Treherbert decorated prior to running the 7.15pm fish and milk train to Swansea. The red, white and blue 'V' on the smokebox was delineated with red lead, white chalk, and a twopenny cube of Reckitts Blue, while the gorse sprigs, completing the engine's VE Day finery, were gathered at Interchange Sidings, Pontypridd, where the train was formed. Passengers on the platforms that the train passed en route were highly diverted by the spectacle and gave Mr Churchill's 'V' sign in reply. *A. G. Powell collection*

Above This photograph, taken at Stormstown Sidings, shows Driver Melvyn Davies and Fireman Viv Crabb in the cab of Abercynon-based No 5686 on 12 May 1953. *V. Crabb*

Below left George Hinton (left) and Jim Williams are at the Graham Buildings, Newport, to take the 'passed fireman' exam in January 1948. Jim Williams, stationed at Radyr Yard Depot, retired as a driver in 1984. *The late Mr G. Hinton*

Below From the *Cardiff Times*, 26 December 1925. *Cardiff Libraries and Information Services*

AGED ENGINE DRIVER.

The death occurred at his residence. Tedworth Villa, Evansfield-road, Llandaff North, on Sunday of Mr Isaac Fricker, a retired Taff Vale Railway engine driver.

Mr Fricker, who was 82 years of age, had only been ill a few days. He was an engine driver on the Taff Vale Railway for about 50 years, and retired some 15 years ago. He was very well known, and was a prominent member of St. John's Church, Cardiff, where he was a sidesman. His wife predeceased him 12 years ago.

Mr I. FRICKER.   He leaves two sons—one of whom, Mr Frederick Fricker, is a partner in the firm of Messrs W. Shapland and Son, timber merchants, Cardiff—and two daughters.

A permanent way gang working next to platform 1, Pontypridd station, circa 1963. *R. Burgess and R. Rose*

A permanent way gang at Nixons Crossing signal box, near Mountain Ash station, circa 1983. Left to right they are Cyril Lethbridge, Billy Stone, Nobby Mahoney, unknown, and Idris Stephens (known as 'Little Id', from Tongwynlais). *T. D. Chapman*

During the research I have done on the Taff Vale Railway over many years, I have met many people and all have helped in one way or another; all have shared a moment of their time with me, whether it be in person or by letter, and this book is a tribute to them. The 'Taff', as the TVR was affectionately called, had many problems to solve but also many employees who helped not only to deal with these problems but who through their own endeavours kept up the morale of fellow railwaymen, through good and not so good times. One such man was John Price OBE.

John was born in 1870 in the small village of Nantgarw, near Taffs Well, and gained employment with the Taff Vale Railway at the age of 11 working with his father, after whom he was named, on permanent way gangs. His father was a platelayer, working from their home station of Walnut Tree Junction (later renamed Taffs Well), and they worked on the section of line from Cardiff to Pontypridd.

In his spare time John made every effort to attend evening classes; his favourite class was art, and he really excelled at freehand drawing. Over time his interests gave him the fundamental skills that he used to great advantage throughout his working life with the TVR and into his Great Western Railway years as well.

On his 14th birthday he went to live with relatives in Ferndale, in the Rhondda Fach, and it was on the TVR's Rhondda Fach branch that he worked as a platelayer's improver, finally becoming a platelayer. He was engaged in the laying of the last part of this branch from Ferndale to Maerdy station, then on to the nearby Mardy Colliery. On 18 June 1889 the opening speeches were heard by

Mr Phillip Powell, platelayer with the Taff Vale Railway, lived at No 1 Taff Cottages, Treherbert, next door to Mr John Price at No 2. Mr Powell lost his arm in a railway accident, but remained employed by the TVR to oil the track points and other less demanding work. He is seen here in the garden of his home with his niece Miss Lillian Powell, circa 1920. *Mr J. Roberts and Miss C. M. Price*

TVR signalman George West is sitting in the garden at No 1 Taff Cottages with his daughter Violet (left) and her friend Charlotte Price, the daughter of John Price, in 1920. *Mr J. Roberts and Miss C. M. Price*

an enthusiastic John Price, but little did he think while listening to Mr G. Locket, the Chairman of Lockets Merthyr Steam Coal Company, that his life would revolve around colliery owners and other such men in the future.

Living at Ferndale enabled John to join the Ferndale & Maerdy United Choir, first as a choir member and later as principal conductor, taking the choir in 1887 to the eisteddfod being held in Caerphilly, and winning the first prize, the coveted silver cup, for the mixed voices section with their rendition of the 'Hallelujah Chorus' from Handel's *Messiah*.

It was during his time at Ferndale that he met a pretty young lady, Miss Jane Williams, and in 1895 they married and moved to the village of

Blaenechau, being blessed with the birth of a daughter in the following year. She was christened Elizabeth, the first of six children, the others being Evan Albert (1899), Richard (1903), Lotte (1906), Margaret (1908) and John (1910).

Fate took a hand in the life of John Price when a vacancy occurred as foreman platelayer on the Rhondda Fawr branch, and he was shortlisted for the job. His employers knew full well about his attendance at evening classes on technical drawing at Cardiff, and this had made him a favourite for the job. So it was that, in bleak winter weather, John, his wife Jane and baby Elizabeth, wrapped in blankets for protection against the dismal conditions, made their way from one valley into another to reach their TVR company cottage at Treherbert, one of a group of four cottages, two being let out to TVR employees and the other two for employees of the Bute Merthyr Colliery.

Moving into their new home under such severe weather conditions must have been a trying time for John and Jane, but as winter turned to spring a warm friendship was kindled between the railway and colliery families, a long-lasting unity between the Powell and Price families. Phillip Powell had lost his right arm while working for the TVR as a platelayer, but was still employed by the company to do less arduous work, oiling the track points for example.

By the summer of 1898 John had joined the Horab Chapel in Treherbert, and this time, in his role as conductor, he took the choir to the eisteddfod at Blaenrhondda to win the first prize, a silver cup.

By 1901 John was working around the newly built island platform at Treherbert station, and on his shoulders he carried the responsibility for laying the tracks. He was helped by the standard line drawings issued by the TVR, but due to certain problems various alterations needed to be made, so using his own initiative, and the skills acquired from his technical drawing classes, he took the responsibility upon himself and put his own changes on paper, laying the tracks and pointwork to match. All went well until the plans were returned, but as no fault could be found, the colliery owners were happy, and the traffic flowed freely without problems, the TVR officials were quick to recognise the special talents of this young man.

By 1902 John and his gangers had cleared the hillside on the western side of Pontypridd station, and had laid a double mineral line clear of the station, but with the introduction of the local passenger services stopping at Pontypridd, problems soon arose with the through Merthyr, Aberdare and Rhondda services. With no sideways expansion possible, it was decided to replace the up and down platforms with a massive island platform containing no fewer than seven platform faces. This rebuilding, together with the extensive work connected with the relaying of the tracks, was slow and careful work that took from 1907 to 1914 to complete.

Pontypridd Junction, situated at the northern end of the station, incorporated some of the most complex crossovers and converging lines on the TVR system, and it was here, over a period of many years, that John established himself as an expert on the complexities and design of track layouts. This knowledge was put to great use when John was given the job of redesigning the Storage Sidings of Penarth Dock, as well as supervising the new lines, or roads, leading to the coal tips. Most of the work was undertaken during weekends, and this meant John occasionally taking lodgings at Penarth.

John and his men were called on several occasions to accidents or derailments on the TVR system, including in 1909 a train from Fernhill Colliery, where coal trucks had been derailed on his own patch at Treherbert. In 1911 they were also on hand, giving much-needed help, at the derailment at the Gyfeillon Coke Oven Works, when a moving passenger train and a stationary coal train collided. This was a sad day for John, as well as for many other people, railwaymen and colliers alike, with the deaths of 12 people, all of whom were known and respected throughout the Rhondda communities.

In 1924 John was appointed Permanent Way Inspector on the lines of the newly formed Cardiff Valleys Division, now under the management of the Great Western Railway, working with the GWR Divisional Engineer, Mr Jim Cunningham. From his office at Pontypridd station, John organised the daily routine of all permanent way gangs throughout the Rhondda, Merthyr and Aberdare Valleys, responsible for the planning and supervision of all major railway projects in the valleys. Also that year, 1924, John was presented with an Illuminated Address, together with a gold medal, watch and chain, by the people of the Rhondda community to mark the achievements of this former platelayer's improver. John was a very proud man that day, and those gifts became cherished possessions, no doubt causing him to reflect many times on his past and the friends he had made.

In 1928 John became a Justice of the Peace, a duty he carried out conscientiously. In 1929 he redesigned the layout at Abercynon, and supervised the installation of a new two-road engine shed there. In 1931 he supervised and installed a new four-road engine shed at Treherbert; sadly, this meant that the former TVR round shed there was dismantled. The latter was

The Illuminated Address presented in 1924 to Permanent Way Inspector John Price. The photograph at the bottom shows him in 1922 working on a musical composition for the local eisteddfod; on the table is a silver cup, a prized possession that he won as conductor for the Horab Chapel choir at the Blaenrhondda Eisteddfod on 31 March 1898. Being a man of deep religious convictions, his musical compositions consisted of numerous anthems and hymn tunes, which in themselves are a lasting tribute to the talents of this man. *Mr J. Roberts and Miss C. M. Price*

situated adjacent to the Lady Margaret Colliery, and its dismantling was a sad day for former TVR employees whose association with the shed had spanned a period of more than 30 years, and held many good memories for John and his men.

In 1935, at 65 years of age and after a total of 54 years of railway service with the TVR and GWR, John Price retired. His final day ended with the return trip from Pontypridd to Treherbert; railwaymen scrambled to shake his hand and wish him well, delaying the departure time at Porth station, and when the train eventually left it did so to the sound of exploding detonators placed on the track to sound a final farewell to this TVR veteran. On arrival at Treherbert John was greeted yet again by many working and retired colleagues,

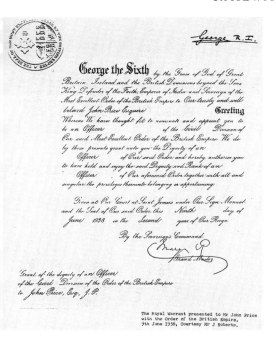

The Royal Warrant presented to Mr John Price with the Order of the British Empire, 9th June 1938, Courtesy Mr J Roberts.

On 9 June 1938 John Price was awarded the Order of the British Empire for services to the local community and to the railways serving the valleys. *Mr J. Roberts*

some from his old gang, themselves retired, all anxious to walk with him to the Railway Arms to celebrate in true railway fashion.

In some ways his retirement was a bit of an anti-climax, as shortly afterwards John joined the firm of Alexander Gibbs as a consultant Permanent Way Engineer; this firm had been contracted by the GWR to supervise the planning and relaying of the Northern Junction at Pontypridd station, together with the link lines and sidings for the newly built Treforest Trading Estate.

During the Second World War John was yet again asked to supervise the relaying of track, this time to the newly built Treforest Industrial Estate Halt, but due to ill health he refused. Mind you, this ill health did not stop him from shaking his fist at German bombers as they passed high overhead en route to bomb the docks at Cardiff or Barry. Most of the time he was unable to see them in the clouds, but it gave him a strong sense of satisfaction to be able to at least shake his fist at these intruders.

After a long illness and with constant nursing from his daughter Lotte, in 1954 John Price died and was taken to his last resting place in Treorchy Cemetery.

NATIONAL UNION OF RAILWAYMEN.

At a mass meeting held under the auspices of the T.V.R. Vigilance Committee held at Pontypridd on Sunday evening last the following resolutions were carried unanimously :—

(1). That this mass meeting of the T.V.R. employees calls upon our E.C. to at once take up with the railway companies for an advance of 5s. per week in wages in addition to the present war bonus and also for an eight hour day as our present wages are not enough to obtain the necessaries of life, and that the South Wales railwaymen meet on Sunday, September 19th, to hear the reply of the E.C. and decide on future action.

(2). That this meeting of T.V.R. employees condemn the unpatriotic and unsatisfactory method adopted by the T.V.R. Co. in reducing the wages of some of the engine drivers in their service seeing that the railways are now controlled upon the regulations of the "Land Forces Act of 1871." We hereby inform our E.C., Board of Trade and Railway Company that inasmuch as the workers are responsible through indirect taxation for the money to reimburse the Railway Companies for any loss on the basis of the 1913 profits, we emphatically and absolutely refuse to recognise the principle of any interference by the Railway Companies or the independent Chairman the right to reduce wages at this period ; and unless a redress of the above grievance is rectified within fourteen days a mass meeting be called of all grades with a policy of "downing tools" to bring this matter to a successful issue.

(3). That this mass meeting of Railwaymen strongly protests against the rumoured intention of the Coalition Government to establish a tax on wages seeing the workers are already too heavily taxed, and we desire to point out that a sufficient increased revenue can be obtained by taxing war profits 100 per cent. and establishing a graduated super-tax on all incomes above £3,000 a year to the extent of 15s. in the £.

Relations between staff and management were not always harmonious, however, and railway trade unionism was active in the valleys, as seen in this report from the *Pontypridd Observer* of 11 September 1915, two years after the NUR was formed. *Pontypridd Library*

A TAFF VALE GRIEVANCE

THE HARD CASE OF MR. EWINGTON, ABERCYNON.

.... of signalmen, guards, brakesmen, and shunters on the Taff Vale Railway was held on Sunday night at the Empire Theatre, Pontypridd. There was a large attendance, and the chair was occupied by one of the workmen, who was supported by Mr Holmes, Cardiff, organising agent; Mr Moses Jones, secretary; and Mr George Maunders (a former signalman at Pontypridd), of the National Society's Offices, London. The customary privilege tickets, we understand, were refused to the men who intended being present at this meeting, and consequently a large number of them drove in brakes from Cardiff, Ferndale, and other districts.

Before proceeding with the object for which the meeting was convened—to consider the desirability of taking steps to secure improved conditions of labour—the meeting unanimously decided to consider the position of Mr Ewington, who has served the company for twenty years. He was engaged as a signalman at Pont Cynon, Abercynon, for ten years, and was a member of the Executive Committee for the signalmen in connection with the last movement. He has been

THE SECRETARY OF THE ABERCYNON BRANCH
of the National Society of Railway Servants for ten years, and has for years taken an active part in Trades Unionism. He is now out of employment, and it is alleged that he has been victimised by the company.

MR. EWINGTON WAS CALLED ON,
and gave particulars of how he had been treated. Three weeks after the collapse of the last movement he was ordered to go to Treherbert. He protested on account of his family, and Mr Harland, while telling him he had been too prominent in labour matters, said he would do his best to keep him at Abercynon.

HE FELL ILL OF RHEUMATIC FEVER,
during which time he was informed that unless he at once proceeded to Treherbert he would have to take his chance of a situation when he recovered. (Angry cries of "Shame!") He saw Mr Harland again, and told him he had been ill, and asked what his position was. Mr Harland replied that he had brought his position upon himself, and expressed surprise that a man with a family like himself should continually cause disturbance among the men. ("Shame!") Mr Harland also said,

"I HAVE NO FAULT TO FIND AGAINST YOU
with regard to your work, but how can you say that you have served the company faithfully when you continually cause disturbance among the men? In fact, I think the whole of your committee, the whole of you men, who cause this disturbance, and put the company to such inconvenience, ought to be discharged." (Cries of "Oh, oh!" and general commotion.) The speaker added that Mr Harland repeated this, pitched into the men about their Trade Unionism, and told him he ought to be ashamed of himself for taking the position he had. Mr Harland also declared that force was used to intimidate the men to join the society,

BUT HE CHALLENGED HIM TO SINGLE OUT
an instance of such intimidation. Mr Harland ultimately told him that, owing to the prominent part he had taken, he had put himself out of the company's employment. He then pleaded to be reinstated in his former position, and Mr Harland asked if he expected to turn away a man who had held that post for three months? He reminded him that he had been cruelly victimised and dismissed after holding the same position for ten years, and Mr Harland's reply was, "Don't blame me. I have those over me whose instructions I have to carry out." (Renewed cries of "Shame!") Mr Harland then told him that the company was dissatisfied with a man in a cabin in the Rhondda Valley, and said that if he applied for it he would have it at a salary of 22s weekly,

BEING 3s. LESS THAN WHAT HE HAD BEFORE,
and that after twenty years' service. ("Shame!") As this was a matter of principle, he placed his case in the hands of the meeting, and would do whatever they decided. (Hear, hear.)

The Chairman declared that it was the duty of all the workmen in the service to protect one who had been so cruelly treated, and said it would be a bad omen for their representatives if they did not protect Mr Ewington.

Mr Holmes said that the men, and not himself, were to decide what to do, and that it was not a matter of intelligence, but of courage. (Hear, hear.) If they had the grit he had always been led to believe they possessed, they would put down tools unless Mr Ewington was reinstated. (Loud applause.) If the meeting believed that Mr Ewington had been victimised, they should pass a resolution emphatically protesting against his dismissal, and appoint a committee to ask for an interview with the directors within seven days, failing which they should issue notices in support of their demands. (Applause.) If they allowed the company to defeat them again, further attempts would be made to knock all the life and activity out of them.

Vigorous speeches were also made by Mr Maunders, who was introduced as "a late victim of the Taff Vale Railway Company," and several others, and, after further discussion, the following resolution was carried with unanimity and with great enthusiasm, the audience, numbering several hundred, rising to their feet and cheering vigorously:—

"This mass meeting most emphatically protests against the action of Mr Beasley in dismissing Mr J. Ewington for being a delegate on behalf of the men during the last movement, and at once calls upon the company to reinstate him within seven days to his former position, failing which notices be signed and issued not later than Monday, August 6th."

A large number present then volunteered to collect the notices in the event of such a step being necessary.

The Secretary explained that a letter had been received from Mr Harland stating that the application sent on behalf of the signalmen, asking for improved conditions of service, would be laid before the directors.

A considerable discussion ensued regarding the position of the guards, brakesmen, and shunters, and it was unanimously resolved to apply for an immediate advance of a halfpenny per hour to each of the three grades, and that in future the minimum rate for brakesmen shall be 22s 6d, and maximum of 25s 6d; minimum for shunters, 27s 6d, maximum 33s 6d; and minimum rate for guards 29s 6d, and maximum 33s 6d.

It was also decided that these demands should be at once presented, and if not granted within seven days notices should be presented, a committee being appointed with Mr Holmes to carry out the work.

Notices will also be given, it was stated, by the signalmen at the same time if their demands be not acceded to.

OFFICIAL REPUDIATION.

The following statement has been made to a Cardiff paper by the officials of the Taff Vale Railway:—

It is quite true that Ewington, as he says, was one of the delegates who in March last waited upon the officials as a representative of the signalmen. In consequence of the representations then made there has been an extensive revision of the classification of signal cabins, under which a considerable number of men have received increases of pay, while no reductions were made at less employed boxes. Shortly after the interviews took place between the delegates and the officers of the company, one of the oldest signalmen at Treherbert expressed a wish to retire on pension.

THE EWINGTON CASE.

AWARD.

In the course of the proceedings which led to the termination of the recent strike on the Taff Vale Railway, it was understood that after the men returned to work the President of the Board of Trade should be asked to express an opinion on a written statement submitted to him whether Signalman Ewington had any reasonable grounds of complaint of his treatment by the company. The opinion has now been given in a letter received by the chairman of the company on Monday as follows:—

"I have carefully considered the question submitted to me on written statements, namely, whether Signalman Ewington had 'reasonable grounds of complaint of his treatment by the Taff Vale Railway Company,' and I have come to the conclusion that, although it was not unnatural for Ewington to have felt that his place was somewhat hastily filled up, yet the final offer of the company to him was certainly liberal, and removed any ground of complaint which might have been held to exist."

Following a downturn in business and profitability, hardline manager Mr Ammon Beasley sought to reduce the company's labour costs. At a union meeting in early August 1900, reported by the *Pontypridd Observer* on the 4th, signalman Mr Ewington complained that he had been victimised by the company for his union activities, and at the end of a noisy session the meeting stated that it 'emphatically protests against the action of Mr Beasley in dismissing Mr J. Ewington for being a delegate on behalf of the men during the last movement, and at once calls upon the company to reinstate him within seven days to his former position, failing which notices be signed and issued not later than Monday August 6th.' Unfortunately some union members struck without giving the appropriate notice, allowing the courts to rule that a union could be sued for damages as a result of it actions. This was the celebrated so-called 'Taff Vale Case'. The second extract dates from 27 October 1900. *Pontypridd Library*

TAFF VALE RAILWAY.

Signal Fitters.

Signal Fitters —20/- to 32/- per week.
Assistants —18/- to 24/- per week.
Hours of Duty —6 a.m. to 5 p.m., 11 hours daily.
Meal Time —1½ hours daily allowed.
Overtime Rate —Sunday Duty double time paid.
Clothing —Overcoat and Leggings every 2 years.

Traffic Department.

Traffic Foremen —37/- to 45/- per week 72 hours. One week's holiday yearly without loss of pay.
Guards —26/- to 32/- per week, 60 hours. 1/- per year advance to 31/- for three years, then 32/- (maximum).
Brakesmen —21/- to 24/- per week, 60 hours, advancing 1/- per year.
Acting Guards —26/- per week, 60 hours.
Groundsmen —Same as Brakesmen.
Pointsmen —18/- to 20/- per week, 60 hours; advancing 1/- per year.
Couplers —12/- to 14/- per week, 60 hours; advancing 1/- per year.
Clothing —Complete suit, cap and extra trousers, 26/- boot money every year. Pointmens' Clothing same as above, 20/- boot money. Couplers', trousers every six months.
Overtime Rate —After 60 hours time and a quarter. Sunday Rate time an a half with a minimum of half a day's pay, and a whole day when time worked exceeds threequarters of a day. For trains ordered out Saturday evening and working until Sunday morning. Sunday rate paid after completion of 60 hours.
Guarantee week of 60 hours when available all the week, providing no unusual interruption takes place, viz, stoppage at Collieries or other interruptions of labour. A bonus of 10 hours paid for Easter Monday and Whit Monday, Good Friday and Christmas Day. No guarantee for rest of week.
Rest —No man called out for duty with less than 9 hours rest.
Numbertakers —10/- per week, 72 hours, No uniform.

Platelayers.

RATES OF PAY PER WEEK.

District.	Foremen.	Second-men and Packers.
Town	29/-	23/- first year, then 24/-
Mining	28/-	22/- " " 23/-
Agricultural	27/-	22/- " " 23/-

Hours of Duty —(Summer 40 weeks).

Monday to Friday	6 a.m. to 5.30 p.m.	Equal to 56½ working hours
Saturday	6 a.m. to 1 p.m.	
Meals	Breakfast ½ hour Dinner 1 hour	

(Winter, 12 weeks). Nov. 20th to Feb. 12th (inclusive).

Monday to Friday	7 a.m. to 5 p.m.	Equal to 50½ working hours
Saturday	7 a.m. to 1 p.m	
Meals	Breakfast ½ hour Dinner ½ hour	

Overtime Rate —Up to 10 p.m., time and a quarter.
10 p.m. to 6 a.m.—time and a half.
Sundays—time and a half.
Fogging Allowance —6d. every 6 hours for refreshments.
Holidays —Good Friday and Christmas Day without loss of pay. When Christmas Day falls on a Sunday such Foremen as have to walk their lengths are paid half-a-day, and for the following day (Monday) when on duty they are allowed a day-and-a-half. Packers and Secondmen are off duty on Monday following Christmas Day without loss of pay, and off duty on Christmas Day (if on a Sunday) with loss of pay.
Clothing —Top coat every 2 years.

Relaying Gangs.

RATES OF PAY PER WEEK.

Foremen.	Second-men.
33/- to 40/-	24/6 and 25/-

Hours of Duty —Same as Platelayers.
Overtime Rate —Sundays time and a half.
Clothing —Overcoat every 2 years. No clothing allowed to 24/6 men.
Holidays —Same as Platelayers.

Ballast Gang.

RATES OF PAY PER WEEK.

Foremen.	Ballastmen.
28/-	24/6

Hours of Duty —Same as Platelayers.
Sunday Rate —time and a half. No clothing allowed.

Signalmen.

Wages —21/- to 30/- per week, 60 hours; according to classification.
Bonus —£1 to £5, according to classification.
Special Rate Boxes —Pontypridd Junction, Penarth Junction, and Cogan Junction, 32/- per week with £5 bonus per annum, Rhondda Fach Junction and P.C. & N. Junction, 31/- per week with £5 bonus per annum. No loss of pay to Signalmen on general holidays.
Porter Signalmen —19/- to 22/- per week, 60 hours.
Clothing —Suit of clothes, cap, and 20/- boot money per annum. Overcoat every 2 years.
Overtime Rate —Time and a quarter after 60 hours worked. Sunday rate time and a half for time worked between Saturday midnight and Sunday midnight. Men called out on Sunday, paid at the rate of time and a half, with a minimum of half a day's pay.
Rest —No man to be called out for duty with less than 9 hours rest.

Lamp Boys.

Wages —8/- to 15/- per week, 72 hours.
Meal Time —1½ hours allowed daily.
Clothing —Same as Signalmen.

Passenger Staff.—Guards.

Main Line —	27/- to 34/- per week, 60 hours.	
Branch Line —	27/- to 30/-	" "
Acting Guards —	26/-	" "
Brakesmen —	24/- to 25/-	" "
Motor Conductors —	25/-	" "
Train Porters —	21/- to 23/-	" "

Meal Times —6 hours allowed per week for Guards, Brakesmen and Motor Conductors. If not relieved for meals, the meal time is to be added to time on duty and to count as overtime.
Holidays —One week allowed without loss of pay.
Overtime Rate —Time and a quarter to be paid for all time over standard hours. Sunday rate, time and a quarter.

Ticket Collectors —	20/- to 26/- per week, 72 hours.	
Platform Foreman —	26/- to 27/-	" "
Platform Porters —	16/- to 20/-	" "

Meal Times —1½ hours allowed daily.
Holidays —Three days allowed without loss of pay.
Clothing —Suit of clothes, cap and extra pair of trousers yearly. Overcoat every 2 years.

Goods Department.

Goods Foremen —	23/- to 28/- per week, 72 hours.	
Goods Checker —	18/- to 22/-	" "
Goods Porter —	18/- to 21/-	" "

Meal Times —1½ hours allowed daily.
Clothing —Suit of clothes, cap and oilskins yearly. Overcoat every 2 years.

Locomotive Department.—Cleaners' Wages and Hours.

14 years of age	9/- per week	12 hours per day.
15 "	10/- "	6 a.m. to 6 p.m.
16 "	11/- "	1½ hours for meals.
17 "	12/- "	*Clothing:* Coat and Sou'
18 "	13/- "	Wester for call boys.
19 "	14/- "	
20 "	15/- "	

Passed Firemen.—(Shed Duty).

Cleaning —3/- per day, 11 hours; 1½ hours for meals.
Labouring —3/6 " " " " "
Firing —4/- per day, 10 hours.
Clothing —Overcoat and Sou' Wester every year.
Promotion to regular Fireman as required.

Extract from an agreement between the Taff Vale Railway and its employees, 1 January 1910. *T. D. Chapman*

Above National Railway Strike Committee of the NUR and ASLEF, Pontypridd and Hafod Branches, September 1919. Left to right, they are: back row, F. W. Dagg, G. Stock, W. Turner, S. Evans, I. J. Dowse, J. D. Morgan, P. Lang, D. Edmunds, A. Selway, C. Robins, F. A. Lewis; third row, W. H. Addis (Assistant Secretary, Pontypridd Branch, NUR), A. Hamblyn, W. J. Nowell, D. Thomas, T. Eveleigh, W. Laubance, T. Evans, A. Sirrell, A. J. Essery; second row, W. Langford (Minute Secretary), W. J. Morgan, D. M. Jones (Chairman, Hafod Branch, NUR), C. Morgan (Secretary, Hafod Branch, NUR), W. Williams (Treasurer, Pontypridd Branch, NUR), A. W. Champion (Chairman, Strike Committee), J Tristram CC (Secretary, Pontypridd Branch, NUR, and Strike Committee), P. O. Gorman (Chairman, Pontypridd Branch, NUR), D. Evans (Secretary, Pontypridd Branch, ASLEF), W. A. Terry (Chairman, Pontypridd Branch, ASLEF), W. Collier (AGM Delegate, NUR); front row, G. Williams, F. Stearn, W. Hayman, O. Morgan, F. Coverdale, G. Lloyd, T. E. Rowlands (Scouts Captain). A. G. Powell collection

51 Years on the Railway

INSPECTOR W. HUTCHINGS, PORTH, RETIRING.

Fifty-one years' service on the railway at Porth, Rhondda Valley, was brought to a close with the 31st of December by the retirement of Inspector William Hutchings, of Birch Grove, Porth. He is a native of Bishop's Lydard, Taunton, and when quite a boy was left the eldest of an orphan family of six children. After working as a labourer on farms at his native village and Bristol, he came to the Rhondda in 1873, being employed in the permanent way department of the T.V.R. In 1892 he was appointed to the office of station inspector, a position which he has since held in an exemplary manner. He is a P.P.G.M. of the Manchester Unity of Oddfellows, and is still a trustee of the Rhys Williams lodge at Trealaw. For 30 years, too, he has been treasurer of the Rhondda branch of the Railwaymen's Sick fund.

In church circles Mr Hutchings has gained honoured distinction by his devoted activities. He is a member of the governing body of the Church in Wales, and is one of the founders of St. Paul's Church at Porth, which was opened in 1887.

Inspector W. Hutchings.

In his interview in the July 1898 edition of The Railway Magazine, TVR General manager Ammon Beasley described the company's pension arrangements:

'On the Taff Vale Railway there is no pension fund, and no contributions are required from the staff. Never the less each and every person is entitled on reaching a certain age to claim a pension according to a fixed scale, the amount of which varies with length of service and the wages received. This great boon to the staff is the outcome of a desire on the part of Mr Guest, the Chairman, to do all in his power to cement the friendly relations which we hope exist for many years to come between the Board of Directors and the great body of the staff.'

Left From the Cardiff Times, 3 January 1925. Cardiff Libraries and Information Services

4. BRIDGES

In his 1898 *Railway Magazine* interview, Mr Beasley described some of the line's engineering undertakings:

'There are some very fine viaducts spanning the Rivers Taff and Ely, the largest being the one at Quakers Yard. Also the large stone arch carrying the line over the Rhondda River has a span of 110 feet and was constructed on a great skew to carry the original line of rail, this being the Brunel-built bridge at Pontypridd. A subway is at present being built under the River Ely to facilitate the communication between Penarth Dock and Harbour. It is being constructed by means of a shield and compressed air, is 10 feet in diameter, and will be lined throughout with cast-iron segments; already about half of its total length has been constructed.

Originally two tunnels existed on the main line, one at Quakers Yard and the other at Ynyscoi, but at both places they have been superseded by open cuttings.

Subsidence caused by colliery workings gives a great deal of trouble and constant vigilance is necessary to prevent any undue subsidence taking place. In fact in some districts this has amounted to three or four feet in one year; consequently the line is now in some places ten or twelve feet above the level of the adjoining lands which at one time it was on a level with.'

This is the TVR bridge over Newport Road, Cardiff, circa 1900 – Queen Street station is on the right and Crockherbtown Junction to the left. In the background can be seen part of the Rhymney Railway bridge that crossed Fitzalan Road and carried the Rhymney traffic to the Bute Docks. *Cardiff Libraries and Information Services*

The old TVR toll bridge at Grangetown, Cardiff, seen here circa 1886, enabled road traffic to travel along Ferry Road, Cardiff Bute Docks, to the Kent Street side. A toll was charged by the Taff Vale Railway from its completion in 1886, which eventually led Cardiff Town Council to build a replacement bridge, the Clarence Road bridge, and the James Street swing bridge. The TVR toll bridge was closed and eventually dismantled between 1892 and 1895. *Cardiff Library and Information Services*

Left This 1862 engraving shows Brunel's viaduct at Pontypridd crossing the River Taff, with the second viaduct of 1862 alongside it. *Pontypridd Library*

Left A DMU crosses the same viaduct on 1 June 1986, approaching Pontypridd station. Through the arches can be seen the supports for the first bridge, built in 1840 when the line was single track. *Author*

Below Near Taffs Well village is this viaduct of Blue Pennant stone across the River Taff. In the right distance of this 27 April 1987 view can be seen the Cardiff Road overbridge, to the left of which is the first site for the station house at Taffs Well (see page 45). *Author*

Top Looking towards Abercynon in November 1984, this is Stormstown Viaduct, crossing the River Taff. It was built to carry the line to Nelson via Ynysdwr Junction, where the Llancaiach line and the Pont Shon Norton spur joined; Ynysdwr Junction is off to the left. Through the arches can be seen the single line that carried the coal traffic from the nearby Dowlais Cardiff Colliery. *Author*

Above In June 1985 the viaduct was demolished by British Rail, a sad day for enthusiasts. Another bridge designed by Brunel, it was really a quite outstanding piece of workmanship. *Author*

Right This is Quakers Yard Viaduct, showing Brunel's 1840 viaduct furthest away and the 1862 extension alongside, photographed in January 1986 looking towards Abercynon (see page 76). Below the photographer is Trevithick's tramway, laid in 1802 and used by Trevithick in 1804; it is crossed by one of the arches nearest to the 'Quaker Yard side'. *Author*

5. SIGNAL BOXES

Moving north up the main line, the TVR-built signal box at Taffs Well station opened in 1921 and was always known as Walnut Tree Junction. The interior was photographed on 24 April 1987, and the box was demolished by Railtrack ten years later. *Author*

This is Maesmawr signal box, at the junction of Llantrisant branch, in July 1985. It was built by the GWR and opened in 1930; it is now preserved at Parkend on the Dean Forest Railway. *Author*

Treforest Junction signal box opened in 1889 and closed on 10 June 1970; it is seen here on 29 December 1963. Located on the main tine, it controlled the traffic using the Exchange Sidings with the Barry Railway. *J. Morgan*

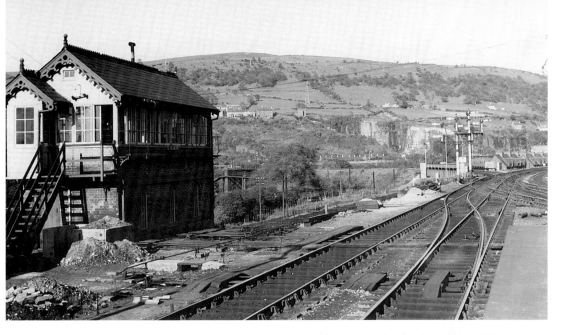

Above This view from Pontypridd station, looking south towards Treforest, shows PC&N Junction signal box on 21 May 1955. This TVR signal box opened in 1888, and controlled traffic using the junction with the former Pontypridd, Caerphilly & Newport line, swinging away to the left in the distance. It closed on 16 June 1970. *The late N. L. Browne, courtesy of his widow, F. T. Hornby collection*

Right Pontypridd Station ground frame, photographed on 6 April 1968, controlled the points and signal on the up main line from No 1 platform into No 2 bay platform (behind the box), and was worked by a member of the station staff as required. Behind the photographer is No 2 bay. *J. Morgan*

Right Pontypridd Junction signal box, seen on 1 May 1971, was the second box to occupy this site (see also page 59). The first was located in the 'V' of the Rhondda (left) and Merthyr lines and opened in May 1887, closing in September 1902. This second, larger, box opened in that month and closed in October 1998. The junction is now worked from a Solid State Interlocking (SSI) panel at Radyr. The discarded rails in the foreground are from the track singling work going on at the time. *J. Morgan*

Left Pont Shon Norton signal box was photographed from the side of Craig Yr Hesg mountain on 1 January 1968. This TVR signal box opened in 1888 and controlled the movement of traffic over the Pont Shon Norton branch from the main line. It closed on 10 June 1970. *J. Morgan*

Below The token is being exchanged between the Abercynon signalman and the driver of a special train, enabling the latter to proceed on to the Aberdare branch circa 1972. The Merthyr line is next to the platform on which stands the GWR-built signal box, opened on 3 April 1932 to replace two former TVR signal boxes, Abercynon North and Abercynon South; it is still in use today. *T. D. Chapman*

Left The interior of Abercynon signal box, with signalman Terry Morgan and station relief Alun Powell having an off-duty chat on 19 May 1988. *Author*

Above The TVR Black Lion signal box at Merthyr Vale opened on 7 February 1871, and was photographed 100 years later in 1971 by the signalman in charge. It was later replaced by a British Railways box (see page 80) from the Llanelli to Cynheidre branch; formerly named Magpie Grove, it had opened in 1960, but the hoped-for traffic on that line had not materialised, resulting in its closure in 1964 and eventual removal to this valley. *Mr Donovan*

Right An interior view of the new Black Lion signal box on 24 February 1988. *Author*

Right Moving now to the branch lines, Nixons Crossing signal box was near Mountain Ash on the Aberdare line. In August 1985, when this photograph was taken, it was past its best and looking neglected. Two months later it was destroyed by fire, deliberately started by vandals on 13 November. *Author*

Left Abercwmboi was photographed in November 1985, looking towards Aberdare. Although in a very neglected state, the photograph clearly shows the TVR design details. *Author*

Left Gyfeillon Upper signal box is seen on 4 July 1968. The open gate gives access to the up sidings of the Great Western Colliery. The box closed on 16 December 1984, and negotiations took place between British Rail and a preservation society to remove it for posterity, as there were by that time so few TVR examples left. However, the box was eventually bulldozed by British Rail in October 1985. *J. Morgan*

Below The rear of Penarth Town signal box on 15 August 1966. This signal box closed in May 1968. *D. G. Thomas*

Aberdare North signal box was also known as Commercial Street by local townspeople. It is seen in 1963, with track repair work in operation. *The late Glyn Davies*

Right Ynysybwl station and signal box were photographed looking north towards Old Ynysybwl Halt on 25 August 1959. M. *Hale*

Below right This is Grangetown signal box, near Cardiff, on 13 August 1966; on the right can be seen the line to Penarth, with a spur leading of to the left towards the Ferry Road branch. *D. G. Thomas*

That brings to a close Volume 1 of this trilogy, in which I have tried to capture the feeling of belonging and pride that the Taff Vale Railway Company, and its successors serving the valleys, gave to their employees. Times were tough and hard, but loyalty works both ways: the railway unions gradually made working conditions better, and the relationship between employer and employee improved. These books are a tribute to those who made it possible.

ORDNANCE SURVEY REFERENCES

The following National Grid references cover the main locations along the former TVR main line between Cardiff and Merthyr Tydfil and the East Branch to the Bute Docks.

Cardiff East Branch Junction	ST188761
Bute West Dock (east side)	ST190757-193747
Bute East Dock (west side)	ST191758-194747
Cardiff West Yard Works	ST190748
Bute Road station	ST191748
Schooner Way railway bridge	ST188755
West Junction canal bridge (between Herbert Street and Schooner Wharf)	ST 187755
Tyndall Street railway bridge (junction of Tyndall Street and Herbert Street)	ST187758
Queen Street station	ST189765
Crockherbtown Junction	ST189768
Cathays BR station	ST182773
Cathays Woodville Road Halt	ST181774
Carriage & Wagon Works	ST177778
Maindy North Road Halt	ST175780
Llandaff station	ST148795
Radyr station	ST135804
Pentyrch Crossing	ST129812
Pentyrch station	ST129812
Ynys road bridge (Heol Yr Ynys)	ST128825
Taffs Well, second station	ST125832
first station	ST129839
Cardiff Road bridge	ST120838
Treforest Industrial Estate Halt (GWR)	ST107862
Tonteg Bank railway bridge	ST098869
Treforest Junction (Exchange Sidings with Barry Railway)	ST083886
Llantwit Road railway bridge	ST083887
Treforest station	ST083889
Goods shed	ST083889
Pontypridd station	ST072898
Northern Junction	ST070902
Goods depot	ST079941
Chapel Street railway bridge	ST073905
Craig Yr Hesg railway bridge	ST076911
Berw Road bridge	ST079913
Stormstown Sidings	ST079941-079936
Carnetown road bridge	ST079943
Abercynon station	ST082947
Viaduct over River Cynon	ST084949
Alexander Place road bridge	ST086952
Incline Top station	ST089955
Quakers Yard Viaduct	ST090963-088964
Quakers Yard Low Level station	ST086965
Mount Pleasant road bridge	ST081978
Merthyr Vale station	ST077995
Troedyrhiw station	ST071024
Pentrebach station	SO070038
Brandy Bridge Junction	SO053051
Dowlais Junction	SO053053
Merthyr Junction	SO052054
Plymouth Street railway bridge	SO052056
Plymouth Street station	SO051056
Viaduct	SO050060-052055
High Street station	SO051061

ACKNOWLEDGEMENTS

I would like to thank the following for their help with these books:

Aberdare Library; Mrs H. Ashby, Assistant Curator, NRM, York; Mr B. J. Ashworth, Lydney; Associated British Ports, Cardiff; the family of the late Mr V. Bishop, Cowbridge; Mr R. Boddy, Cardiff Central Library; Joyce, widow of the late Mr N. L. Browne, Aldershot; Mr L. D. Bryant, Pencoed; Mr R. Burgess, Pontypridd; Mr C. L. Caddy, Weymouth ; Cardiff Library and Information Services; Mr R. S. Carpenter, Birmingham; Mr R. M. Casserley, Berkhamsted; Mr C. Chapman, Hinckley; Mr T. D. Chapman, Cardiff ; Mr E. C. Coleman, Rhydyfelin; Mr V. Crabb, Pontypridd; the late Mr G. Davies, Aberdare; Mrs J. Davies. Pontypridd; Mr M. Davies, Merthyr Tydfil; Mr P. Davies, Pontypridd; Mr Donovan, signalman ; Mr J. Dore-Dennis, Westra; Mr A. Dow, Almondsbury; Mr E. A. Evans, Nelson; Mr S. Fisher, Pontypridd; Mr G. W. Griffiths, Low Ackworth; the family of the late Mrs M. Griffiths, Gwaelod-y-Garth; Mr R. Griffiths, Bristol; Mr M. Hale, Dudley; Mr C. W. Harris, Porth; the late Mr G. Hinton, Pontypridd; Susan, widow of the late Mr P. Hopkins, Pontypridd; Mr F. T. Hornby, North Cheam; Mr G. James, Merthyr Tydfil Public Library; Mr E. Jenkins, Treherbert; Mr D. K. Jones, Mountain Ash; Mr I. Jones, Ynysbwl; Mr P. J. Korrison, Feltham; Mr A. Leaworthy, Pontypridd; LCGB, Ken Nunn Collection; Lens of Sutton Association, Didcot; Mrs H. Lewis, Tonpentre; Mrs H. Lloyd Fernandez, Commercial Assistant, ABP, Cardiff; Merthyr Tydfil Public Library; Beti, widow of the late Mr B. J. Miller, Barry; Mr D. Miller, Cardiff; Mr J. Morgan, Cardiff; Mr B. Morris, Merthyr Tydfil; Mrs L. Morris, Area Librarian, Pontypridd Library; Irene, widow of the late Mr M. Morton-Lloyd, Hereford; National Railway Museum, York; Ordnance Survey Department, Pontypridd; Ordnance Survey Department, Southampton; Mr G. Pearce, Cardiff; Mr B. Phillips, Caerphilly; Pontypridd Library; Powell Duffryn Wagon Company, Cardiff; Mr A. G. Powell, Rhydyfelin; Miss C. M. Price, Treherbert; Mr A. Pritchard, Reference & Local Studies Librarian, Treorchy Library; Mr G. Punter, Cowbridge; *The Railway Magazine*; Mr H. J. Rees, Ynysbwl; Rhondda Cynon Taff County Library Service; the late Mr S. Rickard, Bishopbriggs; Mr J. Roberts, Headington, Oxford; Mr R. Rose, Pontypridd; Science Museum, London; Mr B. Sharpe, Bridgend; Mr G. W. Sharpe, Wetherby; South Wales Police Museum, Bridgend; Mr G. Stacey, LCGB, Egham; Mr D. G. Thomas, London; Mr H. Thomas Pontypridd; Mr C. Turner, Lens of Sutton, Didcot; Mrs K. Warren Morgan, Senior Reference & Local Studies Librarian, RCT Libraries; Mr J. White, Dean Forest Railway, Norchard; Mr F. Winstone, Penarth

INDEX